Copyright ©2019

Anadescha Johnson.
All rights reserved.

The Purity Strategy: A Woman's Helpful Guide to Purity, Confidence, and Wholeness

Printed in the United States of America.

No portion of this book may be reproduced, or transmitted in any form or by any means except for brief quotations in printed reviews without the prior written permission of Anadescha Johnson.

All scripture quotations are taken from the Holy Bible, New International Version, New King James Version, King James Version, English Standard Version, and New Living Translation.

ISBN-13:
ISBN-13: 978-0-9970264-3-6

The PURITY Strategy

TABLE OF CONTENTS

FOREWORD 1
FOUNDATIONAL VERSES 4
INTRODUCTION 5
BRAINWASHED 15
   RETRAIN YOUR MIND 26
      POWER AND AUTHORITY 26
      POWER TO CHOOSE 30
      POWER TO OVERCOME 32
      POWER TO ESTABLISH 34
IDENTITY CRISIS 36
   COMMIT TO SUBMIT 43
   RELEASE THE WEIGHT 47
   ACCEPT THE RENEWAL & ADHERE TO THE PROCESS . 51
   PRAYER: 53
COMPROMISING SPIRIT 54
   DEFEAT THE SPIRIT OF COMPROMISE 68
   THINK ABOUT WHAT YOU ARE RISKING 70
   CONSIDER THE CONSEQUENCES 71
   TRAIN YOUR PATIENCE 72
FLESHLY ASSAULT 76
   PRAYER: 99
DANGER ZONE 100
   GOD'S SILENCE 104
   GOD'S UNFAVORABLE ANSWERS & DIRECTIONS 109
      STABILIZE YOUR FOUNDATION 111
      REFUSE TO SIT IN DEFEAT 112

FIGHT TO REMAIN MOBILE	113
PRAYER:	114
DEATH SENTENCE	115
PRAYER:	122
SEPARATION ANXIETY	123
STRIP IT OFF	128
MISSION IMPOSSIBLE	133
WAR WEAPONS	136
PRAYER	137
FASTING	139
PRAISE AND WORSHIP	140
THE ARMOR OF GOD	142
POSTURED FOR VICTORY	143
PRAYER	146
GENETICALLY MODIFIED	147
KNOW YOUR IDENTIFY	153
REPENT AND FORGIVE	154
SUBSTITUTE	155
TAKE ACTION	156
BREAKING THE CURSE	160
REMEMBERING GRACE	162
THE CROWNING	171
MEMORIES	174
PURPOSE	176
VOW	177
SUCCESS	179
GENESIS	180

Foreword

In our society today, there is one word that is commonly used among people both young and old. What word is this you ask? Sex. Some would refer to it as intercourse or lovemaking. Even though this word is widely used, there seems to be a lack of discussion about it in our churches, and even our homes, today.

There is so much to discuss about this topic and all that it entails. Not to mention the fact that a lot of people are doing it. You might say, "It's human nature", or "God made it for us to enjoy." Indeed! I partly agree with you. Sex was made for us to enjoy, but this was intended only within the boundaries of marriage.

As a teenager growing up in Montel Heights, Nassau, Bahamas, sex was a taboo topic. Yet, the youngest members of my community were still engaging in it. There have been fifteen, sixteen, and seventeen-year-old kids having children due to sex. My mother was one of them; she became pregnant with me at the age of fifteen. Accepting the Lord as my savior at age sixteen was such an amazing encounter for me. However, accepting the Lord did not remove my own desire to have sex; neither did it erase my deep thoughts about participating in the act like many others around my age.

    I knew it was wrong to desire sex being that I was not in a marital covenant, but that did not stop my mind from thinking about it and wondering, *How does it really work*? You also may find yourself at this stage in life. Maybe you want the pleasures of sex or have possibly already experienced it for yourself. I believe that this book will help you overcome the desires of your flesh and give you the tools needed to live a life of purity. Inside this book are testimonies, real-life experiences and principles that will guide you on a road of self-discipline and stability. This is not just another book for single Christians, however. If you are willing to put in the work and apply all the information that you gather from this book, it has the power to free you

FOREWORD

from bondage and remove all the burdens that have been designed to hold you captive.

As you read this book, do it with the understanding that "all things are possible to him that believe" (Mark 9:23). I will believe with you that you will be empowered by God to remain a virgin and to refrain from sex until that appointed day, just as God did with me. Even if you have already engaged in the act of sex, God can renew your purity in the spirit. He allowed me the privilege of standing at the altar at the age of twenty-eight as a virgin to give my husband the free gift of my virginity. If it happened for me, then it can happen for you as well.

It is one thing not to be physically touched and another to have had sex over and over in your mind or heart Therefore, this book is not just about holding your body until marriage but about how to live purified in thought and deed and resist the very appearance of evil. It has been written just for you if you are ready to be free! Open it and receive the process to your life of purification.

Co-Pastor Sheniqua Davis

Foundational Verses

"How can a young person stay on the path of purity? By living according to your word." - Psalms 119:9

"He who loves purity of heart, and whose speech is gracious, will have the king as his friend." - Proverbs 22:11

The grace of God . . .
"Teaches us to say "No" to ungodliness and worldly passions, and to live self-controlled, upright and godly lives in this present age." - Titus 2:12

"Put to death therefore what is earthly in you: sexual immorality, impurity, passion, evil desire, and covetousness, which is idolatry." - Colossians 3:5

Introduction

Many of us are unable to refer to ourselves as "pure" or in right-standing with God, but my question to you is, "Why?" Do you feel as if you have made one too many mistakes? Is there an addiction that has a strong grip on you? Or maybe you feel as if you have fallen so far from grace that it is nearly impossible to find your way back? We have been programmed to think that because we have messed up so many times, we are unworthy of walking in the promises of God. This way of thinking causes us to give up because it seems as if we just can't get it right! But today that battle is over.

    The strategies inscribed on the pages of this book will grant you freedom from the bondage of impurity. No longer do you have to accept that a "stuck place" is your resting place. Through consistency and determination, you can be propelled toward a life of mental, emotional, spiritual and physical freedom. The strategies I share in this book pulled me from a cold place, where I felt alone, abandoned, purposeless, lost and afraid, all as a result of wallowing in impurity. I had people around me but I was still alone.

Even amongst friends, family members and associates, no one seemed to be able or even willing to help me. I felt as if I was on the brink of insanity. I literally felt like my life had no value. Living was not enjoyable for me; I only existed. If you are, or were, in a place where you feel like you are going insane, then this book has the potential to do the same for you–pull you out. If you are anything like me, you are tired of being tired, then let us journey together and fight to get our purity back!

After the excitement of becoming a new believer waned, I faced real-life issues. Issues I never thought I would have to deal with. I had no strategy, and I did not have the strength to push past my feelings to find the answers I desperately needed. I was unequipped and

INTRODUCTION

unprepared. I was void of strategies, void of answers, and regrettably this caused me to drift away from God. As time progressed I wallowed deeper into sin. I became lost, my focus shifted from God to self, and I was in a damaged state. A state where my emotions were all over the place. I had no joy, no peace, no drive and no self-control because I allowed my flesh to run wild. My standards dropped and my wayward thoughts tormented me because now I actively functioned as "damaged goods".

My dysfunctional character and behavior proved that my values were not properly defined or even non-existent. I had a heart issue. Isn't that where all of it starts? The heart is the birthing ground of everything we will face in life. Because the desires and intentions of my heart were impure, this inevitably translated into my life. As I reflect on this time in my life, I am reminded of Proverbs 4:23 which states, "Above all else, guard your heart, for everything you do flows from it." This is what the purity strategy is all about, a matter of the heart. In this book I will offer you the strategies needed to guard your heart so that you can live a life that reflects true purity, confidence and wholeness.

I never thought I would be the person chosen to write about impurity. I was convinced that after becoming closer to God everything would work out just fine, and dealing with hardship and severe testing would be a nonexistent experience. I had no training or knowledge of how to properly utilize the weapons necessary to win. I thought becoming a Christian would be enough. No one told me it required work and that I had to fight to maintain my relationship with God. I surrounded myself with people that were seasoned in the faith. They appeared to be perfect, like they could do no wrong.

Therefore, it was only right that I, too, pretended to be perfect until perfection truly manifested. That is how I once thought it worked. This was an erroneous way to think because pretense never results in deliverance; surrender does. Unfortunately, you are not able to surrender to God that which you pretend does not exist. But I was not aware of this. Pretending to be perfect seemed like the best route to

INTRODUCTION

take. I pretended as if I did not have an addiction. I pretended to be happy, so I wore a plastered smile every day. I pretended to be content while being dangerously miserable and discontent with life. I pretended to be mentally stable while fighting with incalculable amounts of battles.

For a long time, I journeyed on a dark road that led nowhere with my pretense until God's grace shined and illuminated that path on which I walked. Restoration was necessary. With renewed strength, I became resilient enough to learn and exercise the biblical principles of image, purity, growth, purpose, focus, endurance, faith and so much more.

I love the illustration of the formation of a pearl because it directly correlates to my life's journey. The purity of the pearl (my heart) had to be tested. Just as the pearl is the heart and core of a mollusk, my heart is the pearl of my life. Naturally, a pearl is formed when a foreign body becomes lodged inside the mollusk. The animal then senses the foreign object and, as a defense mechanism, coats it with substances as a way to heal.

There are different variations used when categorizing the purity of a pearl: natural, cultured or imitation. [1]

Which variation of the pearl is your heart? Is your heart naturally pure? Or has it been "cultured" by this world and its sinful nature? Or maybe your pearl is an imitation? Are you always comparing your life to another? Jealous of somebody else's portion in life? There have been moments in my life when the pearl of my heart reflected these unsightly variations. I had to decide through the tests of my life whether I would be identified as natural, cultured or imitation.

In choosing to be an imitation or cultured, true purpose can never be established because in the cultivation process you are a mixture or the residue of something else. Artificial entities are introduced in order to cultivate your pearl. But a natural pearl goes through the process without introducing any artificial substances to make it appear more attractive. In choosing to be the most natural, authentic version of yourself, you can go through life's growth processes and

---

[1] Source: https://pearls.com/pages/how-pearls-are-formed

Introduction

effectively journey through purity. Notice I did not say purity destination but journey. This process is continuous.

Like the pearl, your heart will go through a difficult and painful process but the end product promises to be something beautiful and valuable. This process is referred to as the testing of the heart. The Bible says: "I the LORD search the heart and examine the mind, to reward each person according to their conduct, according to what their deeds deserve" (Jeremiah 17:10). Your pearl should have a luster that shines different from any other and a value that increases as you willfully accept the pruning and go through the churning that would rightfully develop your life in every area.

This does not happen overnight. The process requires consistency, dedication, focus and faith. Consistently pursuing all things that are in alignment with living a life of purity. Vowing to remain dedicated to the journey regardless of how difficult the road may get and regardless of the many hurdles that may appear. Focusing on God's ultimate purpose for your life and the impact He sent you to make in this nation. Activating the faith required in order for you to speak to every mountain and command them to move. The faith that keeps you steadfast in knowing that the sovereign God is leading and guiding you.

I was in an empty and confused place where I barely believed in God; my desire for Him seemed non-existent and I could not figure out if I should turn left, right or move backwards. Moving forward just did not seem like an option. I disregarded God, turned my back on Him and blatantly disobeyed Him. I lived every day as if I knew what the next moment would hold. I did whatever I pleased, whenever I pleased, and however I pleased. I made a conscious decision to live a life with no regrets and I disregarded the consequences that would likely follow because of my bad decisions.

I lived a purposeless life for a season. I had a fixed schedule that included school (which I was barely interested in), my then relationship, night clubbing and church when I felt like it or when I was not too tired from partying the night before. This was my "joy" but little did I know, this reckless life was slowly eating

INTRODUCTION

away at me both internally and externally. Only through the help of God and the calling He placed on my life, I now can speak from a place of deliverance. But it was not that simple. I stopped at many roadblocks before realizing that my toxic behaviors and bad decisions were leading me into the pit of destruction.

Soon, I grew tired of the cycles; I was bone weary but my constant defeat and many questions helped me get my drive back and remember the goodness of God. I was sick and tired of hearing another prophesy with no manifestation. I did not need another prophecy; I needed deliverance. Deliverance from bondage. I was bound for far too long by soul ties, generational curses, and all other plans of the enemy and I needed to know how to be free. I then cried out to God for freedom, "GOD! Please hear my heart's cry!" This was my plea. I needed instructions on how to be free, not another word telling me I would be free. I needed strategies. I needed the steps. Get to a place where you become so tired that it pulls you back to the feet of Jesus. Where the flame of your fire can reignite, where your desires begin to burn again for the things of the kingdom.

I write these words to help the young woman who may be going through a chaotic time just as I was, whether it is emotional, physical or spiritual chaos. I want you to know there is much more to life than what you can see or even dream of. God has a plan for your life and His plans are perfect. He is just waiting for you to seek Him first. From my heart to yours, I pray that these words bless you.

I went through an intensive purity process and I am still very far from where I need to be, but I journeyed far beyond where I started. I thought during the process, and even after, that all the pitfalls were unnecessary but if they did not happen, I would not have this story to share with you. I hope that my experience pushes you away from your flesh and gives you a burning desire to pursue God so that He and His grace can establish a sturdy foundation of purity in your life.

Brainwashed

Brainwashed: The act of pressuring (someone) into adopting radically different beliefs by using systematic and often forcible means

There was a point in my life where I thought I was damaged beyond return. My mind was unsteady. It was filled with tormenting thoughts of suicide, self-degradation, not being loved, past hurts and failures and feeling like I was not good enough. Tormenting thoughts of not belonging and thinking I did not deserve joy and happiness. I was discontent with the way my life was going because it seemed as if nothing was going right nor would anything ever go right. Good thoughts were not the norm for me. I was internally disoriented.

At one point I loved God then there were times when I thought loving Him did not make sense. My heart was filled with hatred, unforgiveness and bitterness. I magnified the negatives in my life and that showed through my actions. But that's exactly what it was and where it all started, as "just" a thought. I have experienced a lot of hurts. Being hurt by people I loved who turned their backs on me. Being hurt by giving my all in relationships that left me in an emotional drought. I could not understand why they happened, much less why they had to happen to me.

Many of us fail to realize that most of the things we struggle with are a direct result of our mind. Often we take for granted the magnitude of our brain's potential and function. The brain can construct thoughts and influence behaviors based on what it is exposed to. If this was not so, then we would not have to learn anything but instead we would automatically do the things we wish to do. What is the point of going to school, learning a trade, or being trained for a new job? What would be the point of those things if we already knew how to do it all? This is where learned and conditioned behaviors come into play. The brain is aware of new things by experience, education, exposure and activation of senses (taste, smell, touch, sight and hearing). Therefore, we should be cautious of how we engage the brain in these ways because we are attracted to what we are exposed to. If we were more strategic in what we expose ourselves to, then our outcomes would be more beneficial and effective.

I constantly played thoughts of loneliness and the need for love in my mind. I fixed my mind on and created this burning desire to receive love. These were the seeds I planted in my brain. They then showed through my actions because I freely gave my emotions to anyone in hopes of receiving love and comfort in return. I opened myself up to be hurt because the people I opened myself up to had no desire to aid me in being emotionally restored. Again you are attracted to what you are exposed to. I exposed my brain to desperation and desperation is what I attracted.

The brain is directly linked to the heart. Meaning, if you are not thinking the right thoughts, then your heart will be affected as well. That is why the

Bible states in Matthew 5:28, "But I tell you that anyone who looks at a woman lustfully has already committed adultery with her in his heart." You "look" with your mind because your eyes capture what you see and paint a mental picture in your head.

Therefore, you must censor your thoughts and protect your eye gates and ear gates to guard your heart. I am not just referring to this phenomenon in spiritual terms. According to anatomy, the heart is actually connected to the mind by arteries, veins and nerves within our body. They work hand in hand. That is why oftentimes when the Bible references the heart, it also speaks of the mind and one's thought life. Consider the verse presented earlier about Jeremiah 17:10, which reads: "I the LORD search the heart and examine the mind."

If you can change your thinking, you can change your heart. So then, how is our thinking changed and challenged? It comes by reading God's word. As believers, we should renew our minds and read the Bible on a daily basis, not just when we have a problem or need an answer. That is why Romans 12:2 states:

"Do not conform to the pattern of this world, but be transformed by the renewing of your mind. Then you will be able to test and approve what God's will is--his good, pleasing and perfect will." This relates to the first chapter where we mentioned the different variations of the pearl. We should not strive to be "cultured" pearls, or to have hearts and minds that reflect this world. Instead, we should strive to be renewed and cultivated into God's most natural idea when He first created us, that being purity.

      This goes as far back as the beginning of creation. God created Adam and Eve and He put them in the Garden of Eden with purpose and provision. This was their most natural and pure state but as we read in the book of Genesis, the serpent, the devil, tempted Eve. This caused her to eat of the forbidden fruit, which God had commanded them not to partake of, then she fed it to her husband. They both saw they were naked and exposed. At this moment, sin had entered this world. The peeled hearts became tainted with sin, so then God had to send Jesus to give us a hope and a future.

Jesus is the way back to our most natural and pure state as God intended it to be from the beginning. This does not mean that we are perfect, but the power of Christ works with us to cleanse us from all unrighteousness and to present us without spot or blemish. He does this with God's word, the Bible. God's word is like water and is used to sanctify and cleanse us from all iniquity and sin. That is why Ephesians 5:25-26 reads: "Husbands, love your wives, just as Christ loved the church and gave himself up for her to make her holy, cleansing her by the washing with water through the word."

The enemy's plan is to brainwash and to deceive us as he did with Eve in the Garden of Eden. Brainwashing is an art. Abusers of brainwashing know and understand such artistic dynamics. Whatever controls your mind controls your life. This is why mental invasion and control are the goals of Satan. The enemy is in the crafty business of brainwashing; he uses experiences and societal influences to suppress your ability to think independently. He interrupts your thinking with false ideas he wants you to meditate on instead.

This tactic has long been used in order to keep groups of people controlled. From the 1950s, prisoners of the war were used as the initiators of successful brainwashing. In my opinion, psychologist Robert Jay Lifton described it best. He showed that there were techniques used to control the minds of these prisoners—strategic techniques. He summarized a set of steps used in the brainwashing tactic. Some of which included assault on identity, guilt, self-betrayal, breaking point, channeling of guilt, releasing of guilt, progress and confession.

Ironically, these are similar to the techniques that Satan uses to strategically brainwash us to keep us off track from our destiny. He plays "Connect 4" with our seemingly bad experiences and uses them to our disadvantage. After he has placed us in what he thinks is his perfect position, he then plots and plans his next move. He does this until he has everything in perfect alignment with his ultimate plan to successfully win the game (your life).

The enemy spends time strategically nipping at your identity. He attempts to skew your thoughts toward yourself making you feel inadequate, unworthy, unqualified, average and incapable of ever achieving or obtaining anything more than what is directly in front of you, making you feel so different that you don't belong. He pushes you to play the comparison game and comparing yourself to others will be one of the greatest tactics he uses to assassinate your identity. In our day-to-day lives, we both consciously and subconsciously compare our lives to others.

Social media is the best tool for comparison. Social media is a pro in so many ways but a con in the comparison game. People spend countless hours scrolling and examining the lives of people, not understanding that the things they are viewing are only the parts of people's lives they choose to show. I remember sitting one day trying to figure out why it feels like everyone around me was winning and living their best lives but I wasn't. I messaged my sister about this and her first response was, "That's because we spend too much time on social media." My mind was leading me to measure my life's success based on the people I looked at on social media daily. People wake up and go straight to their phones. In their down times at work, they scroll Facebook, Instagram, Twitter or some other website.

What do we usually see? We usually see people posting their happy families, new successes, new jobs, proposals, marriages, babies, promotions, business ventures, traveling to different countries, speaking on major platforms, a big following of thousands of people. They appear to be functioning effectively in their calling, passion and purpose.

What we don't see are the tears, the family arguments, the divorce threats. What we don't see is that power couple quarrelling because unfaithfulness and insecurities are a norm in their relationship. We don't see that the person who just got pregnant has been battling with infertility for months and years. We don't see the tears because the business seems to be failing and sales are not where they should be or where the owner imagined it would be.

Behind the perfectly functional purpose driven individual we idolize, we don't see the sleepless nights, the feelings of being unqualified, the friends who turned enemies. We don't see all the hurt and the pain behind the lovely pictures, videos and smiles. Remain focused on your own process because you simply do not understand what the person you idolize had to endure to reach their position in life.

The enemy wants you to compare yourself to others; he wants negativity to rule and reign in your life. I was in a season where I unknowingly entertained the thought-provoking lies that the enemy had whispered in my ear. I could not look in the mirror and be content with the image I saw; I was too different so I couldn't help but hope to be like someone else. Someone else who had it more together than I did. This was my daily plea, "God please make me over." I would then present Him with a list of things I needed changed about myself: my height, my lips, my scars, all of my flaws.

I wallowed in defeat because I did not look like others and my life did not look like a success. Nothing seemed to work out in my favor. I based my view of success on things and the life I saw others living. I did not ask God about His success plans for my life. Because I accepted the small seeds that the enemy had planted to distract me, I was pushed to a place of defeat for no apparent reason. Defeat causes you to consistently feel a plethora of emotions–hurt, grief, guilt, anger, depression. It does nothing but distort your image of who God created you to be.

Retrain Your Mind

A pure mind sets the foundation for a pure life. We allow so many seeds to be planted in our minds not understanding the fight that will be required to uproot those seeds. Break the cycle and take control over your mind and your progression in life. This can be a very difficult and tedious process but know it is possible. It took time for the mindset we now have to take precedence; therefore, it will take time for a new mindset to take over. We must strategically go through ways to retrain and reprogram the mind to reestablish a lifestyle of purity. Pure heart. Pure mind. Pure life.

Power and Authority

Power and authority are interconnected but different. Authority is possession; power is = activation. For example, a plug has been given the authority and purpose of charging a phone, but it must be connected to the outlet in order for the power to be activated. That is why authority relates to your identity and power relates to how connected you are to the purpose of why you were created. As believers, our authority comes from our identity in Christ. We are God's children, heirs to an eternal kingdom. We are princes and princesses of righteousness and glory. This is the authority we have because of who we are!

Yet, though we have this authority, we may not have power if we do not know WHO we are or WHOSE we are. That is why the Bible states in the beginning of Hosea 4:6, "My people are destroyed for lack of knowledge: because thou hast rejected knowledge." You must be connected to the source, which is God himself, so that you can come to find your purpose and know your identity. From this mighty connection and relationship with Him, power is activated.

A practical example of power and authority in my personal life is illustrated through my career as a nurse. I have studied to become a registered nurse, and I have gained the authority to be functional in my field of work. Under that authority I have the power to manage ill patients and staff who are assigned to work along with me. But this power would be nonexistent if I decided not to use the authority that was granted to me as a registered nurse. My power had to be activated by putting the authority I possessed into action. The same concept applies to your spirituality.

We were created to dominate the earth; we have been authorized by God to do this. We were given that authority and the ability to activate that power from the beginning of time. God said in Genesis 1:26: "Let them [man] have dominion over the fish of the sea, and over the fowl of the air, and over the cattle, and over all the earth, and over every creeping thing that creepeth upon the earth." How then can we dominate the earth if we cannot grab a hold of ourselves, our own minds? Don't worry; you are not alone. This was me, too. My mind was not my own; it was being controlled by all the negativity I allowed to creep in.

I engaged in activities that left my mind racing, even watched shows that engaged my mind for days after watching. I entertained conversations that were purposeless and bore no fruit. Well, they did bear fruit but not fruits that were edible. The fruits that contributed to mind constraints left me questioning myself, questioning my decisions, and even questioning my salvation. Ever had an experience where what someone said made you question yourself? People would constantly ask me, "What's the point of abstinence? What's the point of waiting? Have you ever bought a car or do you know someone who bought a car without test-driving it first?" I could remember almost every time I sat around a table with this group of people, the conversation left me questioning my reason for maintaining my standard. Like really what is the reward? These conversations were the beginning of my mind being poisoned with negative opinions and theories.

It is imperative that we protect our minds. The power we possess all starts with the mind because what we think of ourselves defines our reality and who we are. Our minds are dynamic, yet fragile, but we do not take the time to understand these dynamics neither are we protective over its fragility.

The body can do nothing without incorporating the mind. Many times we engage in actions we deem harmless because we do not immediately experience the result, but the mind is subconsciously soaking it in and continuously hosting a damage memorial. This was taking place in my life as I constantly allowed people's questions and views to penetrate my mind by meditating on them.

You can maximize not only your potential but also your entire life by filtering your life through your mind. The choice is yours. God gave you that option; He said, "See, I have set before you today life and good, death and evil. I have set before you life and death, blessing and cursing; therefore, choose life, that both you and your descendants may live" (Deuteronomy 30:15 & 19). Take control of your power. You have the power to choose, the power to overcome and the power to establish. Let us explore what these look like.

Power to Choose

"Today I have given you the choice between life and death, between blessings and curses. Now I call on heaven and earth to witness the choice you make. Oh, that you would choose life, so that you and your

descendants might live! You can make this choice by loving the Lord your God, obeying him, and committing yourself firmly to him. This is the key to your life."

- Deuteronomy 30:19-20

You have the power to choose what will reign in your life. Whatever you continuously entertain, especially mentally, will take precedence over your life. I focused on the why's of celibacy and gave power to my feelings of loneliness. My question of "why?" was not being supported by the word; instead it was being supported by worldly views of why celibacy makes no sense. As a result, those thoughts were the ones that flooded my mind every day from the moment I woke up. I went to bed thinking about them and woke up doing the same.

Eventually, I got a void filler for that constant rant of loneliness I was proclaiming. A man. Was He God sent? No, but it seemed so in that season. That directly resulted from what I failed to do, which was choosing what would reign in my life. I allowed mental discontentment to push me out of the will of God for my life. I did not properly use my power to choose. It was my power in deciding to meditate on things that would spiritually elevate me beyond the demands of my temporary feelings.

Power to Overcome

The word shows us that even when faced with temptations that are enticing to our flesh, we also have a way of escape. When you face temptation, know that you can overcome it. Remember: *"God is faithful. He will not allow the temptation to be more than you can stand. When you are tempted, he will show you a way out so that you can endure" (1 Corinthians 10:13).* You have the power to overcome all of your sinful desires.

Jesus won the victory years ago when He was nailed to that cross. All that you could and will ever battle was accomplished through crucifixion. He literally paid for you to be free from anything you would ever think you could be bound by, even the unthinkable. As the blood drained down the cross and drained down His body, your named struggle was in those blood drops.

Envision it. Anadescha's impurity, Anadescha's impatience, Anadescha's doubt . . . all dripping down that cross washed away forever. The same with you!

As He was hanging there painfully, you and everything that could ever be a hindrance to you was being paid for. That right there gives you power. Even though you are faced with it now, know that those blood drops could never be resurrected. They have dried up already. Done away with. So why are you dealing with it might you ask? The enemy sees where you are most vulnerable so he attempts to remind you of that which is already dead. He attempts to use your vulnerability in difficult situations to his advantage. But you now have knowledge of your overcoming power. Use it for your destiny advantage. Overcome whatever you face and use it as a stepping-stone toward your destiny.

Power to Establish

You have the power to establish foundational truths in your life. We choose the direction of our lives by the decisions we make every day. The question is, what direction is your daily decision pushing you in? Are you using your ability to meditate on the problems you have or the truth that will guide you to the possibility of that which can happen? Purity starts with the mind and meditating on the things that can further establish purity in other areas of your life. When we choose to grab a hold of the truth which is God's word and think on those things throughout our day, it becomes a normalcy in our thought process.

Therefore, when you face a difficult situation, you will not be looking for a prophesy or for someone else to encourage you. Edification is necessary. It means to "build up". You will be able to speak over yourself, build up and encourage yourself even when the enemy tries to bring people and things in your way to distract you. That is the biggest investment you could ever make–encouraging yourself. One where you are not primarily interested in validation from others. The word is your guide, not the opinion and views of others.

Be like David who encouraged himself, even after he lost the things that were most valuable to him (his wives and children). By him encouraging himself, he received the strength to first seek God then to go after what was rightfully his in confidence. There will be days when there is only you and God because people turned their back on you. What you stand for will make no sense in the eyes of others because your values do not match.

For moments when you can no longer lean on anyone else, you must practice self-motivation. Motivate yourself to continue to hold on to your values, your truths, the process, and the journey that God has you on. All will not understand but you must establish foundational truth in your life from the word. Stand firm.

Identity Crisis

You would be surprised to know how many people go to their graves without knowing and fully understanding who they are, or who they were called to be. They have journeyed through life, established a name for themselves, gone to the finest schools, or dominated the professional arena, while others may have worked a simple 9-5 just to make ends meet. But when confronted with the question "Who are you," oftentimes these individuals hesitate to respond because they are not sure. I was at a place in life where I could not tell you who I was or who I was created to be. I used my credentials, career and life goals, and other people's views and perceptions of me to shape my identity.

However, after God began to change my heart, I realized that the description I had created in my head existed from things and experiences rather than from

IDENTITY CRISIS

God. My identity was constructed by the names I was called in school, the negativity my family members spoke over my life out of anger, my false view of success and finally old toxic relationships. My character was likened to play dough; whatever you wanted me to be that I became.

Because I was not fully sure of who I was, I conformed to what people wanted and needed me to be. An old relationship of mine serves as the perfect example. I was pressured to recreate the image of someone I wasn't. I already was struggling with my image, so I just needed someone to accept me for who I was. Instead, I had the devastating experience of having my then boyfriend try to transform me into someone else. I do not know if this transformation stemmed from him wanting me to look and act like someone from his past or if it stemmed from him trying to mold me into who/what he imagined I should be. I needed his acceptance so I could not show this devastation.

I vividly remember enjoying fashionable freedom, wearing extensions and makeup, but because my then partner did not agree with it, I stopped almost immediately. I forced myself to wear fewer extensions and less makeup to satisfy him. At that point it was not about hiding who I was, or so I thought. It was things I enjoyed doing. He had a type and a view of what he wanted and he attempted and succeeded at forming me into that person. I agreed to whatever his requests were because I believed it would help our relationship. It was not just about the outer appearance though; he dictated to my speech, my personality, my actions, you name it. In that relationship I was a fabrication of someone else, which made me uncomfortable, but I did what he asked because I thought being myself would not be acceptable to him.

Many times I wished I could do as I pleased but clearly I was not in control of my own life. I felt betrayed. I felt like a prisoner trapped in the life of someone else. I wanted to be in control of the way I looked, how I dressed, how I fixed my hair, my actions and my personality, but instead I cast those desires aside to be accepted by someone who would soon be an experience in the journal of my past. I wrapped my identity in the need to please others, not realizing that this was damaging my very being.

I only realized this after I separated myself from these environments, opened up, and asked God to really reveal who I am because I surely did not know. It is easy to separate from something or someone you do not enjoy but it is extremely difficult when the reverse happens. I was comfortable compromising; comfortable being in what I thought was love at the time. I was comfortable with not having to work past the pain I would have to experience to establish true, lasting change. I *wanted* to stay, but I *needed* to leave. Those same environments were poisoning my identity; therefore, I had to decide between staying in a comfortable yet toxic filled environment and turning to God who gives freedom. Little did I know, the hardest part was not the separation but the process that preceded it.

The emotional devastation that comes with being unaware of your identity is heart wrenching. It feels as though you are renting someone else's body, or as if you are paying rent for an apartment that is severely untidy and uncomfortable with an annoying landlord. Every day you want to serve yourself an eviction notice. How do you give yourself an eviction notice, right? This is how I felt almost every day, the need to leave my body. There is something about having your mind disconnected from your spirit and your body when they should to be in sync.

It is easy to be content with the damage that has already taken place but great joy comes with being able to understand your true identity. If you do not understand who you are, how will you live out your true life? This is an easy target for the enemy to put you in a frame of mind that will keep you spiritually trapped. You are worth a move of God, but know that God never forces Himself on us, we must present ourselves to Him as an open and willing vessel ready to be reconstructed. No job is too hard for God. Our biggest issue is that we have this distorted mindset that forces us to believe that we have to come to God "fixed", not understanding that He is the potter and we are the clay.

Clay in its initial state is not appealing to the eyes, so it needs a potter to be formed into what it could be. If the clay is already a beautiful masterpiece, then a potter would not be necessary. The same thing applies to our relationship with God; it does not matter how we look when we first come to Him but how we end after we have undergone the process. When you first go to God, He does not expect you to be fully formed and developed. This is how I felt. I knew I needed someone bigger than me to help me understand my true self. I knew I needed God.

Unfortunately, I did not think I was "fixed" enough to seek his help. I felt the need to fix some things myself first then and only then would I be qualified enough to go to God. However, He does not need perfection; God knows we were born into sin. While we are covered in sin, God is waiting to shape us into what He really wants us to be, all He needs is the raw material. The clay; the unprocessed, uncensored you.

Pottery must be fired at a temperature high enough to mature the clay; the higher temperatures enable the piece to be hard enough to hold water (http://www.madehow.com/Volume-4/Pottery.html).

When pottery is formed at a low temperature, the pots are highly fragile and porous. Sometimes, in our own molding we still come out flawed, porous and unable to withstand anything, because we refused to adhere to the process.

Many of us abort the process or try to take the easy way out and never complete the process. We do not allow God to complete His work in us. What we have become accustomed to is being memorized by the outcome, the product without considering what it took for the product to look the way it does. We allow our sinful nature to take precedence during the pottery process and although we call it quits, God never quits. He is always there with open arms ready to remold and reshape us until the end product is pleasing to his sight.

Our Heavenly Father ensures that after the rigorous pottery process of helping us to understand our identities in Him, we can withstand the responsibilities He has set here for us to do. Just as the potter has to ensure that the completed piece is hard enough to hold water, God ensures that we will be sustained through the calling He has placed on our lives. Just as pottery must be refined through the fire, we will be tested by fire as well. God needs to ensure that when He pours out, you will have the ability to receive and maintain the outpouring of His blessings. It is all a part of God's desire to show us who we are and help us discover our full potential. Our identity in Him goes far beyond what we could ever imagine but it is a process.

I presented all my imperfections to God, and He was more than glad to walk me through the process of restoring my broken identity and finding it in Him. Below are the steps that God took me through in order to begin the process of finding myself in Him.

Commit to Submit

Submission requires you to die to yourself daily. Galatians 2:20 helps us with this. It reads, "my old self has been crucified with Christ. It is no longer I who live, but Christ lives in me." Our old selves, whatever we were used to, whatever we thought we should be, and the things that we engaged in, were crucified with

Christ. Therefore, we should not be carrying around these things. When you vow to be under God's leading by accepting Him as your savior, His Holy Spirit now lives inside of you. This is something we are not naturally willing to do because there is no willingness to take on someone else.

To be effective and purposeful, we must take on the characteristics of Christ. Taking on the characteristics of Christ requires us to die to ourselves (letting go of the desires of the flesh, leaving behind all that attempts to take the place of God) in order for His ways, His actions, His mindset and His behaviors to be ours. This helps shape our Christ-like identity. Too often we find satisfaction in our sinful state when God is telling us, "Get up, this isn't the life I called you to."

First, you must recognize that there is a need to submit, and that submission comes with benefits. Submission brings about joy, peace, elevation, strong relationships, obedience, and so much more. Submit yourself to God. In order to do this, there has to be a commitment. Commit to lose self to find self. Reflect on 2 Corinthians 4:12, which says: "So then, death is at work in us, but life is at work in you." Total submission exposes us to death. Not physical death but a spiritual death. Just as Christ suffered, we share in that same suffering. The thought of death frightens us because naturally we do not like pain or discomfort. But consider the results that came after Christ's suffering–victory. He paved the way to victory for us through pain.

Our pain comes from dying to our old mindsets, old views of ourselves, who we think we should be, and who people think we should be. This happens so that life, the life of Christ, can be at work in us to transform us into what we were created for. Even though we may suffer, the victory of the cross is active on the inside of us. We leave behind old behaviors and grab a hold of the new growth process that God desires to take us through. Know that the results will always be better. It is a journey through life with Christ for transformation. Often the process of submission to God can feel worse than what the world had you accustomed to. This is what many preachers refuse to tell us.

We have been taught to believe that once you turn from your sinful wicked ways and turn to Christ, you will live a life tiptoeing in a garden of tulips and daisies. I realize that many people are putting on a facade as if this journey with Christ will strictly consist of butterflies and roses when in reality, even though you can experience these things, silence and aloneness might be your portion. Submission requires you to constantly reevaluate yourself and ensure that you are yielded to the guidance and direction of the Holy Spirit. It is your responsibility to take up your cross and follow Jesus. Only you can determine what your cross looks like. Everyone's cross does not look the same; this is why the scripture said take up "your" cross. "Your" is a personal pronoun meaning that it is tapered to a particular person, you, your life. The ERV version of Mark 8:34 states, "you must be willing to carry the cross that is given to you for following me." These statements intentionally use words that show personal ownership.

So, understand that I cannot carry your cross neither can you carry mine which is why it is important to determine what your cross looks like. Your cross signifies your journey, process, growth, sacrifices and purpose. All of these things carry or has a weight, just like a cross.

Let us not forget part "b" of 2 Corinthians 4:12 which states, "life is at work in you." Even though we come into contact with death, life is also at work in you. Although there is the pain of death, with submission there is also the benefit of life. You are now in a position to grow, mature, and come into an awareness of your purpose because now you are in the proper position for use. If you have not experienced the lows of death, then how can you be trusted to experience the wealth of life?

Release the Weight

Weight is anything that hinders your walk with God. The word of God makes it plain, "let us lay aside every weight, and the sin which so easily ensnares us, and let us run with endurance the race that is set before us" (Hebrews 12:1). Admit it, right now you can think of a list of things that serves no purpose in your life;

whether it be people you associate yourself with, things that always come up that were not a part of your to-do list, or just random occurrences.

When you are walking in purpose, there will always be things that "pop up". Know that these things are distractions. Many times, you will not recognize them until they have already distracted you. Distractions will always be present. What are you really doing with your distractions? Are you engaging in them or are you dismissing them in order to focus on your ultimate goal? In releasing all of the unnecessary weight, you will create an atmosphere that is productive. The voice of God will be clearer; when you are focused, you will be more sensitive and in tune with what He is saying and instructing you to do. Shut out the noise; choose to live in peace and progression.

Move forward by leaving it all behind. In living a life of peace and progression, you must give up the things that weigh you down. My relationship weighed me down. It was necessary for me to release that weight. If you have a ton of bricks attached to your hands and legs, then it is evident that these bricks will alter your momentum. Note that a lot of our weight comes from past experiences. I have had people point out certain attributes about me that they used to humiliate me. I had a hard time accepting my image; I was mocked and told that my lips were too big, my forehead was too outstanding or I was too tall. These outbursts caused me to become deeply insecure with my appearance.

Looking in the mirror became extremely difficult because I was not pleased with what I saw. Daily I would look at myself in the mirror scrutinizing my flaws. I played the comparison game all too well: "My friends are much more attractive than I am. Why am I so tall? Maybe I should wear a bang today just to cover my forehead a bit. Why was I created this way? Why does everything have to stand out so much?" I degradingly tormented myself not recognizing that I was doing more harm than good.

The insulting comments and false perceptions of myself stemmed from soaking up all the negative words that spewed from the mouths of people who should not have played a part in the molding of my identity. The emotional trauma, depression and suicidal thoughts are not worth a resting place in your purpose filled life; rise above it. Do not give this negativity the benefit of claiming a space in your life.

Release the labels that were placed on you, the past hurts and the disappointments. In order for you to be filled and come into the knowledge of who you truly are, you have to first cut ties with the identity that you gave yourself. When you give up your life and allow God to grab a hold of it, He is able to do His best work.

Your life is likened to that of a cup; when the cup is filled, no more water can be added to it but when that cup is empty, it can be filled. When you present God with an empty cup, He will fill it up with His truth and His thoughts concerning you. He affirms you, shows you your worth and speaks to who you are. You cannot expect God to pour into a vessel that is already full. He will not force Himself into a little cramped place in your life; He needs a space that He can fully occupy. Release the weight so that you can empty your cup for God to refill.

Today is your day to make a major decision; repeat after me, "Today I vow to never allow anyone or anything to distract or detour me from the plans of God. I will not allow people, negative comments, soul ties or toxic relationships to weigh me down."

Accept the Renewal & Adhere to The Process

God is always willing to mold us into who He wants us to be. The only thing that hinders us is us! Do a self-evaluation right now; ask yourself: *What needs to be renewed in my life? What are the areas that are crying out for revamping? What areas in my life are dead and need resurrecting?*

Renewal is a journey that requires processing; quick fixes are the expectations of those who do not understand the ways of God. Do not give the devil a foothold (Ephesians 4:13 NIV). You took some time, maybe your whole lifetime, to develop this distorted view of yourself; it definitely won't take a day to change what you took a lifetime to create. Do not fret; there is beauty in this process; this process will allow you to reconstruct the areas in your life that have been damaged. Your actions, habits and mindset all need to change; you need a complete overhaul in lifestyle.

These few steps might seem simple to some but they changed the trajectory of my life, and I believe the same can work for you. Remember the process is continuous; we are on a constant journey of learning and evolving. Sometimes you may feel as if you have finally reached the point where your self-love and love for God is untouchable, but remain focused and continue to walk the journey set before you. Continue to read, pray, affirm yourself and declare God's truth. God has been faithful enough to show me little snapshots of my future, and I have been challenged to stay the course.

Prayer:

Lord, release me from the identity I have accepted and allow me to take on my true identity that comes only from you. Renew my mind and spirit; I know that you are willing and well able to transform me into who you created me to be. I take on the process that is required to journey through identity awareness.

Compromising Spirit

Compromise is a mutual agreement reached by the adjustment of two conflicting principles; compromise can be beneficial or detrimental. For example, in a relationship you might have to compromise something you are used to whether it be a habit or a behavior for the betterment of the relationship. There are many people like myself who, in choosing to compromise, lost themselves, their identity, their value and their standards all for the sake of temporary satisfaction.

Detrimental compromise is anything that negatively affects what you stand for. In my life I made too many compromises that were detrimental. I compromised the efforts to discover my true identity by choosing to conform to the identity that others wanted me to have. I compromised my relationship with God because I gave my flesh more control. I compromised my belief in the word because doing my own things seemed to give me more favorable results. I compromised my desire to wait for my husband to engage in sex by giving into pleasing a man who did not have the same goal as I did. Better yet, he had no desire to live according to the principles of the word. I compromised my standards in relationships because I became impatient with God. Waiting was not something that satisfied me even though it was crucial.

    I recall sitting in my room and writing a list of traits I wanted to see in my future husband. I wrote nearly two pages in my journal that night and I was so confident that God would grant me my heart's desire. The list I created was filled with superficial desires. I had more details about his appearance than the posture of his heart and his character. I needed him to be tall, dark, well-built and handsome. I needed him to be well dressed. All of these desires were okay but they should not have been the root of what I was interested in.

    I never thought for a moment that my heart's desires might not be in alignment with God's plan.

Many times we come up with these plans for our lives without consulting God first. Is He not the source of our being? He knows everything about us, so what happens if He does not support your "list"? Or what if that time you have set in your mind is not his perfect time? God has no issue with granting your heart's desires. The issue arises when we go outside of His will trying to do things on our own, in our own time and by our own might.

In moments like these, reflect on the following: "Delight yourself in the Lord and he will give you the desires of your heart" (Psalms 37:4). This scripture gives us simple instructions. Find great joy in and take pleasure in God and He will grant you your heart's desire. I have heard this scripture quoted many times but nine times out of ten, people only mention that God will give us the desires of our hearts while failing to mention that there is a prerequisite. The prerequisite of delighting in God, which means to truly find peace and fulfillment in Him over anything else.

When you are in proper alignment with God, His desires become your desires. Too often we want

God to do what we say when in actuality it is supposed to be the reverse, us doing what He says. Many times we do not consider God; we organize our own agendas then include God. We as humans are also guilty of waiting until our backs are against the wall to incorporate God into our plans. The next time God does not honor your list of needs, consider this: He just might be protecting you from the dangers your finite vision does not permit you to see.

Now may not be the right time for that particular need to be met; you just might be in a season of pruning and preparation. God may be saving you from wasting time on things that are not a part of His purpose; He always has a greater plan. Consult God regarding every area in your life, your relationships, career choices, ministry and every other area. Ask God to help you operate in obedience so that His perfect will is done in your life.

I initially decided mind that I would honor God and wait until He brought me someone I could do life with. I was tired of playing the trial and error dating game. I discovered a newfound confidence after leaving my last relationship, which left me physically and emotionally drained and spiritually disoriented. About six months after I got saved, I remember praying, "The next person I get into a relationship with is going to be my husband." That night I gave my relationship desires over to God and the journey to embrace my single season began.

I walked around with my head held high knowing that in due time God would present His best to me. I no longer focused on my relationship status; I was more focused on getting closer to God, finishing school, traveling and enjoying life. People often would ask, "Why are you still single?" or "When will you find a man?" Those who knew me would make statements like, "I really want you to find a man" or "you have been single for so long". It really did not bother me; I just prepared myself for the many questions and comments. This became so routine till I had my answers on speed dial.

Have you ever been to this place? Where the comments and the opinions of others did not matter because you were so set on the promises of God? I would say, "Whenever God is ready, whenever He sends him my way" or "I'm good; I don't need any added stress. Let me enjoy my freedom while I can." My answers were genuine. I was confident that God would allow my mate to find me at just the right time.

Have you ever felt this way? Where you felt pressured by those around you to do something you were not ready for? Or had friends and family who would always ask when are you going to get married, have kids, find a job, go to school, make more money, get a home? They ask these questions so many times that it probes your insecurities and causes you to start second guessing yourself, second guessing God's plan for your life and second guessing your journey.

Readiness cannot be forced; it requires preparation. Timing is everything. A lot of times we are pressured into doing things without properly evaluating what is required to sustain that which you have rushed into. God's blessings can easily look like a curse when you are ill-prepared to effectively handle what He has blessed you with. Refuse to miss your blessings by being forced into doing something outside of its season.

Prepared was something I was not. I knew that my present heart's posture was not one that was prepared to openly welcome someone. I was not ready to handle God's best. I know that my attitude would have pushed Him far away; I knew that I was not spiritually grounded enough to handle a mate along with trying to maintain a steady relationship with God. Years later, my strong sense of confidence to wait on God slowly faded away and discontentment crept in.

Impatience moved me from the feet of Jesus and pushed me to do my own thing. I moved from a place of desiring for God's will to be done in my life to a place of questioning His will. I would ask: "God, I think my single season is done. I am ready to meet my husband. I am ready to start my family. Why is it taking so long? Why hasn't he found me yet? Years have passed and I'm still single; when will this end? I am tired of being alone." This was my daily cry.

Amid confusion and frustration, I met someone who looked the part. The audition seemed fitting; the counterfeit was bought, as it appeared to be the real deal. I even went back to the list I wrote years ago and voila we had a match! As we got to know each other, I felt uneasy about the entire connection but I looked past my uneasiness because he matched the list. We continued to talk but a little voice in the back of my mind kept reminding me of the prayer I had prayed years ago for my next relationship to be my husband.

Even though he fit the title perfectly, the uneasiness I felt kept me from agreeing to add an official relationship title onto whatever we had. But I still continued talking to this guy and then after a month or so, I finally prayed about him. Funny how I got this far by choice, did what I wanted to do and then brought God into the equation after willingly proceeding with something He did not sanction.

I prayed but I did not open my ears to hear from the heart of God. At this point I had already moved so far away from Him that I did not know what His voice sounded like anymore–the danger of willingly following the voices and demands of your flesh. I took, what seemed like, God's silence for approval and that pushed me to move further and further away from Him. God never stopped talking; I just stopped listening. My ears were open but not receptive. My flesh took precedence over my soul.

My unwillingness to seek God and wait pushed me into the arms of the enemy and manifested His plans in my life. His plan was to plant me in a disastrous environment, one that sought to deceive me, move me away from the feet of God and keep me trapped. The connection with this guy was the enemy's trap. I became so caught up in the connection that I sometimes forgot that God existed. My prayer life dwindled. I went to church but was never present in church. I say that because I was spiritually disconnected. My connection to that guy was my idol, my god. The enemy's plan was temporarily achieved because of my disposition with God.

Our relationship was not strong enough to withstand trials; it was comparable to being a babe in Christ. During my season of waiting, I felt like God was taking too long, so I compromised my standards for temporary gratification. Once you have set standards for yourself, do not allow anyone or anything to cause you to compromise. Ask yourself: "Does my decision fall into the category of the detrimental compromise as mentioned?" Satan would lead you to make hasty decisions for temporary satisfaction that will result only in permanent damage.

Carefully consider your actions and ensure that they are in proper alignment with God's will. Impatience is one of Satan's greatest tactics; he will try to frustrate you and get you to believe that your waiting is in vain. I compromised my standards and lost the fight not only because of impatience but also to satisfy others. A disaster is waiting to happen when you lower or adjust your standards to suit the pleasures of someone else's. In my life I experienced many disasters that left me feeling depressed, anxious, hopeless, suicidal, discouraged, purposeless and disgusted. All of these emotions visited me, and tried their best to end my life.

I have realized that people all play a significant part in adding extra, unnecessary hurdles in our lives. Or on the contrary, sometimes people come into your life to add value and help develop you in different areas.

People are placed in your life for many reasons: to assist you, help guide you, mentor you or simply test you. Decipher what roles the people in your life are playing. If someone threw you a pop quiz that you did not prepare for, chances are you will fail! If you give someone free access to your life and you are excited because they seem so cool and you have gained just another friend, you have already failed the test. What if Satan sent that person to disrupt the plans that God has for you. What if their intent is to distract you from your purpose by falsely engaging you for years in order for you to waste time?

There are many encounters I had with people who were a complete waste of time and energy. The connection looked good in the beginning but as we journeyed, they could not add to my life in any way, shape, or form. As a result, they began to take away from my life instead. Connecting with these persons stripped joy and the ability to trust away from me. As I shared dreams and visions with them, they stripped hope away from me because in their minds either I was dreaming too big or I was not being realistic. Therefore, it is so important to remain in tune with the voice of God and allow His Holy Spirit to give you His discerning spirit. Some people should have never been a part of your life because of their impure intent to destroy you.

The Holy Spirit is who guides your life and guides you into all truth. Remember John 16:13, "When the Spirit of truth comes, he will guide you into all truth. He will not speak on his own but will tell you what he has heard. He will tell you about the future." He gives you insight into the future. The Holy Spirit is necessary in our lives because He helps us stay the course by giving us not only hope but also direction. But He can only be that authority in your life if you allow Him to be. You give the Holy Spirit authority by delighting yourself in God and willfully feeding your spirit. This magnifies your relationship with God.

The reality is, if you are not constantly feeding your spirit man, it will die–the same applies to the flesh. If you constantly feed it, it will flourish but if you do not nourish it, ultimately, it will die from starvation.

Unfortunately, this is not a one-time experience. I wish that we could just take part in a ceremony or a ritual where we kill our flesh and that's it, game over! But this is a daily process. Luke 9:23 states, "Whoever wants to be my disciple must deny themselves and take up their cross daily and follow me." If you desire to be a follower of Christ, it requires work and effort.

You must deny your feelings, thoughts, your desires and everything else that is not pleasing to God. You take on the efforts it takes to pursue the things of God daily regardless of what it feels like, regardless of the pressure you may feel and how heavy your cross may get. Every day you must put your flesh under submission so that God can be glorified.

Submission to God requires you to be set apart from the world. It is difficult to stand out and be a true representation of yourself if you are fighting to fit in with the crowd. Jesus said, "I have given them your word; and the world has hated them because they are not of the world, just as I am not of the world. I do not pray that you should take them out of the world, but that you should keep them from the evil one" (John

17:14-15 NKJV). We are not of the world but instead sent to the world for a perfect purpose. Fitting into the world was not God's intent; He intended for us to be purposeful while being protected in a world that we are in but not a part of. Our citizenship is that of the kingdom of God. You must be distinguishable from the world.

Your flesh will tell you to stick with the crowd (the world); it creates this environment for you to be comfortable, which entices you and eases you into sin. If you are in a choir, no one will know your true voice because they only recognize one sound, the sound of the chorus. Yet when you decide to do a solo, people can recognize your unique voice. People will begin to appreciate your sound. This happens when you step into the uniqueness of what has God created you to be.

Step out of the crowd even if people refuse to accept you. Refuse to compromise your identity to fit in. Refuse to compromise your values because of discontentment. Refuse to move and decide without approval from God. Refuse to rely on your emotions and your sinful nature to be the guidance you need for your life.

The following steps help to make better decisions when I am faced with a compromise:

Defeat the spirit of compromise

If there is anything I have learned throughout my journey, it would be to never compromise yourself for anything that would cause destruction of your beliefs and character. We push ourselves in the way of harm unknowingly, and sometimes knowingly, but carefree of the consequences.

First, you must discover what you compromised and why. What lie did you entertain? What bad thought did you meditate on? If you do not do this, then you risk continuously falling into the same traps that led you to compromise in the beginning. You must be honest with yourself. Find out what you compromised with and write them down. Find spiritual truths that would correct the lie you believed. For example, for me,

I told myself that God was taking too long to reveal my mate. I thought He had forgotten about that being a desire of mine and I grew impatient. I meditated on the following scriptures to counteract these thoughts:

"There is a time for everything, and a season for every activity under the heavens" - Ecclesiastes 3:1

"It is not for you to know the times or dates the Father has set by his own authority." - Acts 1:7

"Let us not become weary in doing good, for at the proper time we will reap a harvest if we do not give up."
- Galatians 6:9

"Do not be anxious about anything, but in every situation, by prayer and petition, with thanksgiving, present your requests to God." - Philippians 4:6

You do not have to choose multiple scriptures. You might need only one. Decide every day that you will revisit those truths and meditate on them. It is my prayer that as you meditate on these truths, they become a part of your thought process.

As you spend more time with the word, remember James 1:22 (NLT) which says: "Do not just read and listen to God's word. You must do what it says otherwise you are only fooling yourselves." It is purposeless to know and not do. Live out what you meditate on. It is our responsibility not only to study but also to apply the word of God to our daily lives. You will find that the application of the word of God will inevitably bring destruction to the spirit of compromise. I am not saying that the thoughts you have will automatically become null and void but your faithfulness to the word would supersede the desire to compromise your standards and your calling.

Think about what you are risking

Many times we sanction our flesh to do things we sometimes do not even think about. Think about it; if you carefully thought about everything you wanted to do before you did it, the outcome would be different.

You would be able to evaluate the outcome and weigh out the benefits if there are any. In doing this many negative thoughts would never manifest into actions. But many of us live recklessly. We get an idea and we are quick to act on it whether it be good or bad because we do not count the cost. The danger in this is that it will cost you something. Are you willing to give up your salvation for reckless living for the sake of temporary pleasures? Are you willing to give up your peace, your purpose, God's will for unbeneficial temporary satisfaction? Are you willing to risk everything for a romantic evening under the stars with a bouquet of roses and a candlelit dinner with the enemy called flesh? Count the cost.

Consider the Consequences

Compromise results in risking your values and respect. Trust me, people respect you more when you adhere to your values. It may appear that someone accepts you when you give into things that would compromise your values but it is actually the complete opposite. If you say you stand for something, then you must stand for that. People will single you out, outright envy you, and maybe even abandon you but they will know you. They will cease from asking you to do certain things, go certain places, and engage in certain activities because they will know your response before even asking. You will be labeled and singled out but your values will be secured and established. Be bold. Refuse to compromise for the sake of acceptance. Be set apart even if it means being alone.

Train Your Patience

"You get the chicken by hatching the egg, not by smashing it open." –Arnold Glasow

The key to everything is patience. Even the chicken has to go through a proper birthing process to become a chicken. Someone's hastiness to want to get the chicken before its time by smashing open the egg will not speed up the chicken's birthing process.

Instead, by smashing the egg they would have caused it to abort the chicken's birthing process. This is the same with our lives. Attempting to speed up the process by doing unfavorable things will not grant you any success. It will cause you to miss your lesson and delay your growth. With patience you will see the right fruits at the end of the process. Impatience causes you not only to rush but also to abort the process.

Impatience damages the self, relationships and progress. Your progress, your miracles, your breakthroughs are all on a timer, but the only person who knows when that timer will sound off is God. Do not be discouraged; there is divine beauty in not knowing. If you knew when everything would take place and how it was going the take place, then you would not need God. You would not need His promise. Wrapped up in the beauty of not knowing is your growth; your character is being developed, your faith is expanding and your relationship with God is being strengthened.

To get these benefits, we must train our patience. Patience is a skill. In training your patience, you are required to wait, learn and embrace your current situation. When you become anxious, remember the word of God, which is filled with His promises. It also requires being content with where you are. Contentment does not mean that you are settling but that you are embracing all that your current position has to offer. There is beauty right where you are but you can't see it because you are distracted by where you desire to be. In singleness there is beauty. In marriage there is beauty. In success there is beauty. In failure there is beauty. In abundance there is beauty. In lack there is beauty. There are valuable lessons in every season of your life.

There is so much to learn in your current position but we are so eager to move that we oftentimes miss out on valuable lessons. Missed lessons cause delayed growth. In life, you will not progress if you do not grow. Your position might change but your growth level will remain the same. That is still deemed a suitable criterion for being unsuccessful. There is no point in elevating if your elevation would still result in dysfunction. Embrace the lessons of your present rather than rushing to a future for which you are ill-prepared.

    Don't get me wrong. Embrace but don't settle; there is a difference. To embrace means that you accept willingly and enthusiastically.[2] In settling you become comfortable and complacent. We miss so many important moments and opportunities because of discontentment and impatience. How can God use you if you are trying to move from the very place where He needs you to be planted? Pain is never comfortable but comfort never precedes breakthrough.

---

[2] Source: https://en.oxforddictionaries.com/definition/embrace

Fleshly Assault

The battle is not yours! No really, it's not. Everything that you fight against can be handed over to God. The Lord Himself will fight for you. Just stay calm (Exodus 14:14). This is a difficult concept to grasp when you are going through a rough season. Was there ever a time when you felt as if you did not understand the things you do or why you do them? I sure have, on numerous occasions.

Paul explained it best, "I don't really understand myself, for I want to do what is right, but I don't do it. Instead, I do what I hate" (Romans 7:15). I felt this; I could not really understand myself. I would have a strong desire to do what is right but just when something occurs that was a temptation, I would do exactly what I did not want to do. The church, in my eyes, did not help too much with this. By the church, I mean people in the body of Christ. I would always be told by believers that I needed to stop doing this and stop doing that but never "how". No one ever answered the question, "How do I deal with not giving into my temptation?" Through journeying with God, however, He showed me how.

That is why it is so important to have a personal relationship with Him. A lot of times, the Holy Spirit will be the one to teach you things that man cannot. People are quick to judge your situation, but many of them do not have the patience to disciple you through it. When that happens, know that God is there and He has the wisdom you need. James 1:5 reads, "If any of you lacks wisdom, you should ask God, who gives generously to all without finding fault, and it will be given to you." There is nothing in this Christian walk that you should face alone.

God is with us and will never leave us. He will lead you and show you what to do. It is also comforting to know Jesus can relate to the battles and temptations that we face as feeble human beings. Hebrews 4:15 states: "For we do not have a high priest who is unable to empathize with our weaknesses, but we have one who has been tempted in every way, just as we are--yet he did not sin. Let us then approach God's throne of grace with confidence, so that we may receive mercy and find grace to help us in our time of need." It is encouraging to know Jesus can relate to our struggles. They persecuted him, so they will persecute us also. Yet, as the scripture says in Hebrews 4:16, we are given grace and mercy in our time of need. There is hope for your situation!

Before knowing this truth, I felt as if I constantly battled and battled alone. Sex was my battle. The condemned word amongst believers. I blamed it on my weaknesses not understanding, at first, that it was a battle that I needed to be intentional about fighting. Sex outside of marriage is a norm in the world; it is done so carelessly. Not only in the world but also in the church. We just do a better job at hiding it. This is in no way bragging about sexual sin because it is not in alignment with what we should profess as citizens of the kingdom of heaven. But! It is among one of the many struggles that believers deal with. I did! Many times as believers this is a difficult struggle to share because it is such a taboo subject in the church.

Therefore, the issue is rarely addressed. If someone shares it in search of answers, then the response would be something like, "Read the word; just stop doing it; pray." Journeying through this process had me fearful not because I thought someone would find out but because I was jeopardizing my purpose. I did not want to be another church hypocrite who said one thing and did the opposite in secrecy. But I did not know how to break free. The only way out was through God. It took more than just reading the word and praying. It took strategy. Strategies that helped revamp my thought process. Strategies that helped grab a hold of my flesh and make it obey God. Strategies that helped me move away from environments that were toxic to my growth process.

Even though the world considers sex outside of marriage a norm, it easily could tear you apart. It entices you while engaging in the act but the aftermath is not worth it. Many people would say this is not true but many people do not relate the issues they deal with to sex. They try to relate it to something else or blame their issues on someone else. For every person you have had sex with, you carry around a part of them because you have participated in an act that connected not only your bodies but also your spirits. There were many times I acted out, said things I would not usually say, did things I would not usually do. God helped me understand that I took on the character of the previous sexual encounters I had. This is the danger of soul ties.

When you have a soul tie, you deeply join with someone and you begin to struggle with what they struggle with. You did not have an addiction before but now you have a craving for something you previously had no interest in. Think about the trend. Envision this scenario: You never get healed from your soul being tied to one partner but that relationship ends. After some time you proceed with another relationship and the sexual relations start again. This is now a new soul tie on top of the old one. How many soul ties do you have? Granted this was the trend for multiple relationships, how many soul ties would you have? You see the danger?

Sex is carelessly engaged in because it is such a worldly norm but the price you pay is expensive. It is a temptation, yes, but falling into the temptation costs you something. Temptations are inevitable and we are presented with them every day. We are tempted to lie, gossip and cheat. We are tempted to settle because of the fear; we are tempted to do so many things contrary to God's will but interesting enough temptations directly result from what entices your inner you. James explains it best: "temptation comes from our own desires, which entice us and drag us away. These desires give birth to sinful actions. And when sin is allowed to grow, it gives birth to death" (James 1:14-15).

Even though temptations are inevitable, your response to temptation makes the difference. Giving into temptation is what gives birth to sin. The danger behind this is that sin is progressive. Continuously watering your sinful actions (by watering I mean practicing) causes you to develop habits that are constructed to make sin become the norm in your life. As this is happening, your spirit is dying because two different trees are not allowed to grow in your soil at the same time. Your soil is your life. Either you are watering your soil with the word and other practices that would push you toward God, or you are watering it with sinful practices that will pull you away from Him. It all stems from your response to temptation. Jesus was tempted yet He did not sin. The best response to temptation is patient endurance.

> "God blesses those who patiently endure testing and temptation" - James 1:12

The real battle was between my flesh, which is my sinful nature, and my spirit. I responded to the temptations with my flesh. I gave in and was controlled by the desires of my flesh. You know if you are living by the flesh or by the spirit based on the fruits you produce. When you operate in the flesh, the results are always negative. Fruits of the flesh are impatience, greed, thirsting for things that are not pleasing to God. The word clearly outlines what it looks like to live by the control of the flesh compared to living in the freedom of the spirit. Galatians 5:19-21 reads*:* "The acts of the flesh are obvious: sexual immorality, impurity and debauchery; idolatry and witchcraft; hatred, discord, jealousy, fits of rage, selfish ambition, dissensions, factions and envy; drunkenness, orgies, and the like." In addition, "but the fruit of the Spirit is love, joy, peace, forbearance, kindness, goodness, faithfulness, gentleness and self-control" (Galatians 5:22-23). Your fruits reflect what is really going on within.

> *"A good tree cannot bear bad fruit, nor can a bad tree bear good fruit."* - Matthew 7:18

Your fruits determine what is overtaking your life. The flesh can overtake your life but only if you allow it to. We see this every day, the lifestyles of people who are being controlled by the flesh. It appears as though they are living their best lives by having causal sex, abusing substances and engaging in drunkenness, clubbing, or any other excessive behaviors. We can get into the habit of envying these people because their lives seem to be so enjoyable, so carefree and lax, but we do not understand that their habitual sin will eventually lead to destruction (death). You may think I am being a bit extreme but no, it does not always have to be physical death. There are many people who we see every day, communicate with, and even journey through life with considered to be among the "living dead". Spiritually and emotionally dead!

    I went through a season of professing out of my mouth that I was a believer while being spiritually dysfunctional and emotionally battered. At one point the battle between my spirit and flesh intensified and my flesh completely controlled my life. I felt stagnant, immovable, unusable, unworthy. I engaged in things that satisfied my flesh such as lusting and sex. I was struggling because I gave into what my body wanted. Sex was a void filler for the love I needed to experience. Conversation with the flesh went something like this: "Sleep with that guy, you know just once, and you will be satisfied. I mean since you like him and all, it won't hurt. We only need to get rid of this craving."

    I attempted to get rid of my sexual cravings and was successful for a while but I did not fully understand the depth of the sin I was committing. I did not know one sexual act would turn into a continuous pattern of dysfunction. I was stuck in my mess and after each encounter I woke up feeling emptier than the time before. Internal conversations would often sound like: "Hey! Flesh! You did not tell me I would feel this way." I constantly engaged and entertained conversations with my flesh instead of using that same energy to seek and talk to God.

    This is a daily fight. If you do not see it as such, then you will wake up and go through your day being unprepared. Unprepared to go to battle, unprepared to deny yourself, unprepared to take up your cross, unprepared to overcome. We must prepare ourselves every day by putting on the armor of God. This is a spiritual battle and the Bible instructs us to "Put on the whole armor of God, that you may be able to stand against the wiles of the devil" (Ephesians 6:11). As a result of being ill-equipped, I came in contact with an ungodly soul tie.

    My toxic love affair became a soul tie. This particular guy was attached to me in ways that I could not explain. He was like a drug that I needed, a drug I felt like I would suffocate without. When battling a soul tie, you are well aware of the fact that you should not be connected to a person for whatever reason but you are unable to let go of the relationship. You have connected with a person sexually and your soul interprets that connection to be permanent, not understanding that it is only temporary.

See, your soul operates by principles and there is nothing you can do to deter that operation. Your soul knows God ordained sex for marriage; therefore, if you have sex, your soul thinks you are married. Its impossible to think that you can say to you soul You cannot sit and say, "Hey soul, even though I am not married to this man, can you just hold off on that deep connection thing that you do so I could have this fling right quick?" No! It does not work that way. Your soul listens to and operates by principles.

Sexual impurity is just that dangerous. This is why the word tells us in 1 Corinthians 6:18 to "Flee from sexual immorality. All other sins a person commit is outside the body, but whoever sins sexually, sins against their own body" (NIV). The NLT version says to "Run!" from sexual sin. The war will try to consume you daily. It is you against your flesh because most times you are not considering or thinking about your spirit man, so it becomes a non-factor in your fight.

Soul ties are difficult to shake because you are trying to rid yourself of someone who you connected with intimately, who satisfied the thirst of your flesh. When you are thirsty, sometimes you go through any means of relieving that thirst. You search for the well that you once drank from, for that burning desire and thirst to be quenched. When you constantly feed into the flesh, it leads to so many consequences and feeling undeserving of God is one of them.

Condemnation results from feeding the flesh. You will feel like you deserve nothing good because in your mind you believe you have messed up too many times. While I was feeling the sting of condemnation, I did not seek God; I could not seek him. I felt like I was not deserving of God. I fluttered in shame and I could not dare open my mouth to God after I had failed Him so many times. What made it worse was that I kept failing in the same area; I shed countless tears, had anxiety attacks, repented, prayed, even fasted. But still no change. After all of this, I felt like God was tired of me, tired of me getting it wrong. So, what did I do? Stop talking to Him. This is exactly what happens when your life is led by the flesh.

The flesh dictates to your feelings; it makes you feel dirty. Your flesh persuades you into thinking God cannot hear you because of the state that you are in. The reality is, God wants us to surrender it all to Him so that He can renew and restore us to who He desires us to be. Romans 8:1 states, "There is therefore now no condemnation to them which are in Christ Jesus, who walk not after the flesh, but after the Spirit" (KJV). It takes a lot to push into living a life in Christ after you have sinned so much, but in Christ is the only place where you will experience true freedom from condemnation. God calls us to be free.

Condemnation caused me to pull away from God and this took a toll on our relationship. My relationship with God was almost nonexistent. I did not search for or seek Him. I even lost my conviction which was the worse it had ever gotten. I had reached a point where I sinned freely without experiencing any conviction. That is a dangerous space to be in. Conviction pushes you to want to change, do better and not engage in sin. Conviction comes with the presence of the Holy Spirit. Because my relationship with God was in a drought, I was not in tune with His Holy Spirit who would have given me direction and convictions for my sinful habits.

    I walked a dead life for a season. A season that was longer than it should have been as a result of making bad decisions. I tried to rush past the single season I was in because I was "lonely". I filled the void and emptiness I felt with relationships and sex. Satan uses any open door available to manipulate and deceive you into situations that would satisfy you only for a moment. My dead relationship with God was his entrance but in the midst of it all, God was with me and He is with you, too. Even though your life may feel like a valley of dry bones described in the book of Ezekiel in the Bible, it does not have to stay that way. Those dry bones can come alive.

The unquenchable thirst for sex will increase and you will continue to fall into the trap if you do not confront your sin. Your void filler can become your addiction. I willed not to have addictions of any form but I allowed a temporary position to push me into actions that would cause semi-permanent damage. Mentally I thought I was losing it but physically I was content. Spiritually I was lost; emotionally I was unstable. There are not too many words to describe the torment I felt. There were days when I felt completely exhausted. Mentally I was so unhealthy that it bled out physically in the form of depression, anxiety and unexplained headaches.

I remember sitting on my bed one night and sieving through all the mistakes I made that had pushed me to my current position at the time and suddenly I caught an anxiety attack, gasping for air, crying, feeling as if right then would be my last few breaths. But I wore the best mask whenever I had to leave the house because I needed everyone to think I was okay and that I had life all figured out. Inwardly I was shattered; outwardly I masked it all in perfection. A compilation of mess. Know that it is okay to not be okay. This is the constant cycle we go through when we live controlled by the grip of the flesh.

A cycle is like a circle in that it has no end, but options still exist. You have the option to break that thing that has no end. You have the opportunity to pierce that thing and create your exit. Remember: "The mind set on the flesh is death, but the mind on the Spirit is life and peace" (Romans 8:6). When you set your mind on the spirit and functionally operate in the spirit, God gives you peace, freedom and the strength you need to overcome the cycles that once kept you bound.

When you expose your spirit to fleshly desires, it is like being trapped in a smoke-filled room; it suffocates you. The enemy is so crafty and now I understand why the word advises us to:

"Be alert and of sober mind. Your enemy the devil prowls around like a roaring lion looking for someone to devour. Resist him, standing firm in the faith, because you know that the family of believers throughout the world is

undergoing the same kind of sufferings."
- 1 Peter 5:8-9

Satan is strategic in his tactics; therefore, we must be strategic as well. He uses strategies to plan your downfall, and you need to use strategies for your victory. Satan waits for the right time; he waits until you are most vulnerable to lure you into sin. The enemy does not want you to live by the principles of the word because he is afraid that you will walk in your true purpose and become a menace to his kingdom.

You can have what the word of God promises but you have to remain alert and do what the word says. Being alerts means you are watchful. You will sense an attack, or an error from a mile away if you are alert. If you are not alert, then attacks could sneak up on you and wreak havoc in your life. Be in tune with the Holy Spirit; He is our protector and our guide, when danger is approaching, He will send you a signal. Your connection with God is of utmost importance, so stay connected; stay alert.

FLESHLY ASSAULT

Have you ever been in a season where you were mentally and emotionally tired of being beat down by the pressures of life? I had no fight left in me and I decided to stay in the mess I was in. I felt like God had forgotten about me, forgotten the things He had promised me. I lost my hope. I lost belief in God and in myself because of disappointment after disappointment.

Though I did not fully understand it then, I know now that God was trying to build up my character. I missed the purpose of that season because I was caught up on being temporarily satisfied. In your most uncomfortable state, *God is doing His greatest work. Understand that your discomfort is the birth passage to your purpose.* Too often we are caught up on how we feel and constantly complain because our situation is not working out how we want it to.

Focus is especially required in tough seasons. What you focus on makes the difference in the outcome. Focus on what God is trying to do in your life rather than focusing on the dissatisfaction you feel or the disappointments you have been facing. Many times the disappointments are intentional methods that God uses to show us that we need to focus more on Him. That we need to rely more on Him rather than our own abilities or the abilities of mere humans. Inevitably, what you focus on is what you become. Your mindset constructs the tone for your environment and your current state of being. Therefore, you have the power to change your reaction to your circumstances by adjusting your focus. Are you fighting your battles with the sword of the spirit or are you succumbing to the flesh?

> *"Fix your thoughts on what is true, and honorable, and right, and pure, and lovely, and admirable. Think about things that are excellent and worthy of praise."*
> - Philippians 4:8

Now is the time for us to run after a lifestyle of purity and holiness; now is the time to stand firm in your beliefs and free yourself from all fleshly activities. During the pursuit of purity, we sometimes feel the need to immediately cut off things we deem "bad". We check off things like drinking, smoking, sex, stealing and lying and automatically feel like we have accomplished the optimal lifestyle of purity. This reminds me of surface cleaners. If there is a rug in the middle of the floor, then most times the first instinct would be to sweep the top off while leaving the hidden dirt underneath. Although no one will see it, the dirt still sits under the rug you refuse to lift up.

    Dealing with surface issues are fine until they resurface and the experience is worse than before. I enjoyed surface cleaning; it was not a very tedious process. I maintained a level of comfort but eventually the issues resurfaced and tormented me. I experienced more heartache because I brushed over the issues in my life instead of digging up the roots that grew from the contaminated soil I lived in. A good tree's roots are planted deep within the soil. Just as it takes time for the roots to pierce deep into the soil, it takes time for us to develop new habits.

    Unfortunately, we refuse to take the time to understand that there are precursors behind every habit. Before anyone forms a new habit, they must practice a consistent set of actions. Your daily practice of this habit inevitably strengthens the root. This applies to any habit you possess, whether it is good or bad. Deal with the root, not the fruit. The fruit often appears as the most appealing part on the tree but the fruit is only the result of what someone has already planted.

This brings me back to our first point, dealing with the matters of your heart. What does your heart look like? The residue of your heart's truth bleeds out through your words, actions and your lifestyle. Do not be distracted by the things that will not bring you victory. Focus on the things that will propel you toward your destiny. You must first determine what your destiny should look like.

Who would really be interested in digging in dirt to see what the root of a tree looks like? It is much easier to pick the fruit and enjoy its savory taste. Maybe you are like me who felt disconnected from her father and because of the neglect, you unknowingly sought love from intimate relationships to feel love and secured. My affection barrel was empty from childhood, and I needed that void filled. Maybe you are a victim of abuse, molestation or abandonment; take time to discover what drove you to develop an ungodly lifestyle and habits.

We sometimes fail to understand why we act or respond the way we do. Our responses may be a reflection of the events that have taken place in our life. God's best work is revealed when we acknowledge that we are in need of a great work.

Pruning is the most difficult part of the process, with the many moments of falling short, sinning and feeling like no one can save you from your sinful state. I was brainwashed into thinking that because I had sinned habitually, I was disqualified from God's grace and deliverance.

I referred to myself as a failure because I could not seem to get my life together. Now I know that a person only fails if they stop trying. I used my quest for success to mask the pain I felt. Truth is, success is only measurable in God's eyes but if we are outside of Him or disconnected from Him, then we would continuously chase that which we think will satisfy us.

I, like many others, desired the finer things in life thinking it would make my life better. Only through connecting to God did I realize that all the answers I needed were in Him and nothing else. The pain I experienced was a result of the dominance of flesh that superseded everything else in my life. Really, who else could have revealed that to me?

Make your flesh obey God. Be so focused on God that you cause your own flesh to commit suicide.

Prayer:

Heavenly Father, I pray for a flesh that obeys your will. I bring my body under submission to you and I ask that you have your way with every part of me. My body is your temple and I desire for you to live within me. Help me make my environment conducive enough for your dwelling. In your name, Amen.

Danger Zone

High risk, controversial, hazardous!

What do you do when God is silent amid your storms? How do you react when God tells you "no"? Or better yet, what would you do if you asked God for direction and the direction He sent you in did not lead to the destination you expected it to? What if He gave you, what you consider, unfavorable instructions? Consider Jonah. God gave him specific instructions to deliver a word of judgment and repentance to the people of Nineveh but Jonah ran away from God. Jonah stepped into the danger zone because he did the opposite of what God had instructed him to do. He experienced calamity and through his calamity he cried out to God who was merciful to him. After receiving mercy he decided not to run away any more but instead go to the city of Nineveh where God had sent him. Through his obedience he was instrumental in helping to save the lives of many.

Looking back on the patterns of my life, I now realize that the unfavorable pressure I experienced escalated when I stepped outside of the parameters of safety and walked into a danger zone. My parameters of safety meant staying under God's covering through obedience. I wanted the relationship but God said no. I needed answers regarding God's direction but got silence instead. There were desires I had that were not met because I refused to obey what God instructed me to do.

The enemy whispered defeat in my ear and I allowed his words to cripple me. When we experience defeat, we become tired, overwhelmed, exhausted and subsequently worried. There were a few points in my life where I felt as if things would never get better. It seemed as if everyone around me was getting blessed besides me. I prayed, fasted, read the word; I did everything right, well, so I thought, but everything still went wrong. I felt like God was not listening to my requests.

The only thing that was left for me to do was scream and cry, which I did and that did not work either. During that time, I was enrolled in college and failed most of my classes that semester. Furthermore, during what I thought was the worst season in my life, it seemed there were no answers. Still, I attempted to seek God for direction.

God told me what to do regarding college at that time. So I listened carefully and followed His instructions and it still seemed as if nothing was working out. Or was it? I cried, "God you told me what to do. I did it but I still came out defeated! Why?" This was when my belief in God started to diminish. I concluded that I might as well do my own thing thinking that even when I try to do right I still lose. It only made sense, right? Wrong! I allowed what I thought was God turning His back on me to tarnish my belief in Him.

What do you do with your defeat? What if God does not work it out the way you imagined? Would you

Danger Zone

still worship and acknowledge Him or would you turn away from Him like I did?

God's Silence

Sometimes silence can feel like absence. In my life I had many instances where I thought God was absent. In seasons of financial lack. In seasons where I was so deep in sin I needed His presence. In seasons where my relationship with my biological father was practically nonexistent. I prayed and asked God to "show me an open door, tell me how to get out, show me that you are here with me, and assure me that you will take me out of this mess that I am in." I just wanted a way out.

I prayed and prayed and nothing happened; now I was sure that had God left me to fend for myself. I honestly cannot remember Him answering any of those prayers. I wanted God to rescue me from my discomfort but I now realize that rescuing me was not His will for that season. I needed the discomfort; I needed the pain to grow. Being rescued was my will, not God's, and because I was so focused on what I wanted, I got distracted by my own wants and ultimately missed the lessons I needed to learn in that season.

My will did not match God's will. It is now evident that He wanted me to stay in the heat and endure the process so I would progress. Still, I failed that test, over and over again. In those moments of unanswered prayers and silence, I thought God was absent but He was there all along waiting for me to get closer to Him. When God is silent, know that He has not forgotten about you. Remind yourself of this truth daily because the enemy will try to persuade you into thinking God does not care or that He has forgotten about you. Satan will persuade you into thinking God has turned His back on you.

In God's silence, He is trying to teach you something; stay alert and remain prayerful. Trust that even in His silence, He is doing a great work on your behalf. Sometimes we become so familiar with God that we forget who He really is and how much we need Him. Before I experienced any kind of hardship, my journey as a believer was going fine. The problem is, I started to become comfortable. I had to realize that it was my responsibility to draw closer to God, to seek Him deeper, to pray more, to fast even when I did not feel like it. I had to get out of my comfort zone and become hungrier for God. I needed Him then, and I still need Him today. My desperation and brokenness increased my desire to seek God and I knew He was the only one that could fix me.

In my season of experiencing God's silence, I did not wait well. I waited in frustration. My focus was not on growing or learning anything; my focus was on getting out. I just wanted out! I often would cry out, "God why won't you understand that I just want OUT!" He did not respond to my plea, but I am assured now that it was only because He wanted me to grow. Unfortunately, in those moments growth was not on my mind. So I moped, sulked, threw pity parties until that position became my resting place.

While you are waiting for God's perfect plan, develop the spirit of submission in total solitude to God. Many times, we submit our wills to other areas and give God a portion but when we are in total solitude with God, we are operating in the right posture of submission to Him. Understand that God's agenda is never to push us away from Him but to always pull us closer. Be intentional about how you wait; do not take matters in your own hands! Consider Job 13:14: "Why do I put myself in jeopardy and take my life in my hands?"

Sometimes moving away from God can make you feel like you have accomplished something that God couldn't. We prefer to find things that temporarily bring comfort instead of waiting on God to answer. It might appear to look good for a while until the odor seeps through. When we allow our impatience to push us to a "fix it yourself" state, there are consequences. This happens when we move from the feet of God. We are no longer in tune with His desires or His heart. The enemy is so crafty; He takes His time and allows us to experience fake contentment and happiness in the beginning of our mess like when I willfully invested my time into a man who God never intended for me. In the beginning it felt right. I thought I couldn't be happier, not understanding it was false happiness and contentment.

As humans, when we operate in a body that is ruled by the flesh, it inclines us to react to our environment. When God is silent and things in life are not going our way, we begin to focus on everything that is going wrong. The hardships we experience start to become a part of our thought process and the enemy tries to make us feel that this is how it will always be. He pushes us to meditate on our downfalls, shortcomings and defeats so that we can disconnect from God.

The enemy understands that when we are disconnected, we cannot experience growth. In seasons and times like these, we have to be intentional about not entertaining the thoughts that magnify our problems. Instead, we must seek God, even in apparent silence. Are your responses natural or spiritual? Ask yourself this question. Choose spiritual responses that will push you to seek God regardless of the circumstance–a spiritual response of prayer that is unconditional.

God's Unfavorable Answers & Directions

Sometimes what we equate to God being silent is Him not really giving us the answers we are looking for. Many times God would give us answers and because we do not accept it as what we need, we feel as if He is not speaking to us. We ignore His voice and think, "This can't be God". No, it is Him; He is speaking to you but you have selective hearing. On the contrary, when we go to God, many times we go with a plan already in our minds. Not only does this create confusion but also unnecessary disappointments. Why? Because when things do not go as planned, we get angry with God. We create our own hurts.

First, we need to sit and see what His thoughts are concerning a particular situation before we make our personal requests known. Too often we make it about what we want, how we want it and when we want it. When God's answer is "no", it might have a different meaning, as we usually would hear. Sometimes "no" is outright "no" without any deviations; other times "no" means "not right now." Whatever God's answer is, even if it is "no", know there is always a purpose behind it. Your vision is limited. God is omnipotent. He knows all things and sees all things.

God's direction is never unfavorable but we sometimes perceive His direction as hostile and critical because we fail to fully understand His nature or His heart. Our faith is not rooted deeply enough in Him. If it was, then we would understand that even when God's way is tough, His plan is perfect. You would know that there is glory to be revealed through your situation.

Although it is difficult, generations and nations will be impacted and saved because of your willingness to follow God's plan. "For I know the thoughts that I think toward you, saith the Lord, thoughts of peace, and not of evil, to give you an expected end," Jeremiah 29:11, reminds us that God's promise still stands even when things do not make sense. This assures us that even when it looks or feels unfavorable, you are right where you need to be, once it is in line with God's plan.

All God wants us to do is submit to His will and His ways and everything will be okay. Disregard your fickle feelings and depend solely on God; He is unchangeable. When faced with difficult situations, let your first instinct be to trust God. This helps us remain aligned with God. We must get back in position.

Here are some challenges you can use daily:

Stabilize your Foundation

Through all the ups and down of what I have experienced, the one thing I lacked was stability. I was like the house built on the sand; my foundation was not strong enough to withstand the storm. Not even the smallest rainstorm. Ensure that your foundation is stable by building it upon the rock–the word of God. There are no faults in the word of God. Through your storms, trials and tribulations, God's promises still remain. If you are unaware of this truth, you will have nothing to stand on. Believe that the word of God applies to you today and that the promises are yours to experience.

Refuse to Sit in Defeat

When you sit in a place of defeat, you welcome that defeated state as your reality. You meditate on the problem and all that can go wrong instead of believing, hoping and knowing it will work out for your good. Meditating on mountains (struggles) you feel you cannot move will distract you from the truth. In reality you must believe, by faith, that you have the ability to climb over mountains or simply speak to it and it shall move. In Matthew 17:20, Jesus said, "I tell you the truth, if you had faith even as small as a mustard seed, you could say to this mountain, 'Move from here to there,' and it would move. Nothing would be impossible". Sitting in a place of defeat distracts you from your true abilities. You can conquer every battle you face but that all depends on how you are fighting but more important who is backing you up.

DANGER ZONE

Fight to Remain Mobile

Make up in your mind that you will never become stagnant again. You will not allow the struggles of life to paralyze you or paralyze your belief. Keep moving even if you are not able to visualize any benefits. Sometimes your rewards are hidden because God wants you to trust in Him instead of trusting in people and material things. Trust that He will guide you, even in darkness. Trust that He will be a lamp to your feet and the light that illuminates the path He created you to walk along.

You will achieve strength, endurance and growth through the pain that comes with pushing beyond your feelings. When you feel as if you cannot go on, know that is when you have the most strength. God assured us that His strength is made perfect in our weakness (2 Corinthians 12:9). We have access to His strength. Take advantage and use what is rightfully yours.

Prayer:

God help me stay at your feet even when it seems unfavorable. Keep me planted in the foundation of your nourishing soil. Help me not to allow discomfort to move me away from you. Help me understand your will; your will for me to grow and continuously progress in you. Continue to remind me that in the silence you are still present. Let your strength remain perfect in my weakness. Give me your eyes so that I can see past what is right in front of me and be able to see what you are doing in the spirit realm on my behalf. Great are you Lord and your sovereignty reigns above any other. Let this truth always be in my life so that you remain a priority. In Jesus name, Amen

Death Sentence

The fact that you are reading this book means that you are alive. According to Satan I was not supposed to be alive today. I wanted to commit suicide. I often drove by this particular stop light and my mind would try to convince me to speed into the opposite way of traffic. The enemy kept planting seeds in my mind trying to convince me to end my life seeing it was not getting any better for me. But can I tell you that the purpose for your life is far greater than any temporary feeling you can ever feel or any temporary season you could ever experience? Seasons change! Your hard season will soon change.

The enemy hoped that death would have been the penalty for my many sins. My ungodly relationship was one thing he hoped would aid in my death. After fighting to overcome sexual sin and losing repeatedly, I felt defeated, and I accepted that defeat. I felt like I tried everything but nothing worked. This was the mindset that Satan wished for me to have because it pushed me to think I could never recover. Suicidal thoughts overtook my life because I continuously told myself that I could never be an asset to the kingdom of God. If I was not an asset, what then was I? A complete waste of existence, so I thought.

I experienced a continuous war in my heart and in my mind. Life made no sense because I was so crippled by the grip that sin had on my life. A grip that I felt could not be loosed. I did not truly live life because my vision was clouded with sin. This is why the world urges us to flee from sin. It negatively affects us in more ways than what we can imagine.

Thank God for grace. Whatever you went through that was meant to kill you did not work. The enemy hoped that you died as a penalty for your sins. The sins he influenced you to commit. I should have been dead right now; that was His plan. I should have been cramped away in a corner suffering from some sexually transmitted disease; that was His hope. The pregnancy scares had me shook. I should have been a single mother struggling to make ends meet; that was His desire. This is not in any way bashing single mothers but God knew I was not fit to sustain that battle. Single mothers are superheroes but God knew that was not my superpower. He allows you to go through battles He knows you can win with His help. Satan gets excited when your life looks like it is going the way he planned and his desires seem to be getting fulfilled. Satan's hope is built on our failures. Our failures fuel him to push harder in order for him to deem us qualified for the death penalty.

Despite all of your impurities, God was purifying you through them all. I know that makes no sense and it sounds like an oxymoron, but that is the heartwarming reality. As a child of the King, you have direct access to kingdom privileges. Satan knows this and therefore his goal is to distract us from what we have access to. Remember, when you know your identity, you recognize your authority, and through being connected to the source, you activate your true power and potential.

According to John 10:10, it is Satan's plan to "steal, kill, and destroy."

Steal. Steal your joy and cause you to wallow in defeat because even though you tried to make it right over and over again, you failed terribly. You failed miserably. Depression kicks in because you think you can never move beyond your failures. You feel as if you can never overcome once you have fallen.

Kill. Kill your dreams and ambitions. Damaging your sight by causing you to lose hope in all things good. He attempts to kill all hope and belief that your life could ever get better. He wishes for you to believe that your life will always be one filled with defeat–sin, failure and struggle–so that you will remain stuck.

Destroy. Destroy your faith, trust and belief in God so that His promises would seem unreachable and ultimately impossible for you to never to live a life in pursuit of destiny and purpose. Faith empowers you to triumph over what you see. Satan wants to destroy any ounce of faith that you can ever have so that your sight is fixed only on what is directly in front of you.

Death Sentence

Even though Satan's plan is to steal, kill and destroy, God's plan and purpose is for you to have a rich and satisfying life–an abundant life.

"The thief does not come except to steal, and to kill, and to destroy. I have come that they may have life, and that they may have it more abundantly." - John 10:10

"The thief's purpose is to steal and kill and destroy. My purpose is to give them a rich and satisfying life."
- John 10:10

The destiny of your success lies dormant inside of you. We tend to hinder our success. We do this by magnifying the imperfections in our lives rather than focusing on what God's destiny for our life is. Magnify your strengths instead of your weakness then watch the transformation. You only accept the death sentence if you accept your failure as a failure. If you see your failures as successes or lessons, then you will have no choice but to get up and shake the dust off and move forward. Everything, not some things but everything, works together for the good of those who love God. Use that promise as your fuel. The fuel that will drive you beyond Satan's death scheme that is to keep you stuck. Grab a hold of truth. Take advantage of your promises; they are there for you to use.

What you have experienced was just purposed pain. A pain that would be the fuel you need to go after your purpose like never before. Pain that would be transformed into a message and a testimony that would help others walk in freedom. This is what it was for me. Even though I thought the sins I committed would take me out and would always be counted out, God had another plan. His will and purpose for my life is greater than the death plans of Satan. He gave me new strength and the renewed faith I needed to overcome. Faith that subdued kingdoms, worked righteousness, obtained promises, stopped the mouth of lions, quenched the violence of fire, and escaped the edge of the sword (Hebrews 11:33-34). Faith that turned weakness into strength.

Death Sentence

Many tried to stand against you but God was before you. His faithful promises are your armor and protection (Psalms 91:4). You felt the heat, but you did not get burned. God shepherded you. He shepherds us. In John 10:11, Jesus refers to Himself as the good shepherd. We are His sheep. As a good shepherd to us, Jesus laid down His life for us (His sheep). He watches over you day and night. He protects you from the attacks of the enemy. He ensures that the weapons that form against you never prosper. He is concerned with everything about you.

"I am the good shepherd. The good shepherd lays down his life for the sheep. The hired hand is not the shepherd and does not own the sheep." - John 10: 11-12

"I am the good shepherd; I know my sheep and my sheep know me—just as the Father knows me and I know the Father—and I lay down my life for the sheep."
- John 10: 14-15

Prayer:

God help me not to become a prisoner to the thing you have called me to trample over. You created us to overcome. Help me to be intentional about learning the lessons that are necessary to enhance my growth. On days when I feel the weight of life on my shoulders, remind me that every difficulty I am faced with will be used for my good. I will not become weary when life gets tough and it seems like the enemy is winning but instead I will trust you. I know that Satan will always be defeated. I reject his plans and I call to life everything you have for me.

Separation Anxiety

Separating from the sins that had me bound was difficult because I was comfortable there. I found comfort in the sin I committed. But I was more afraid than comfortable. Fear gripped me. I thought about how I would be publicly humiliated when I turned away from certain things and people. I thought they would be thrilled at squandering my name and further crush the Christian community for being fakes. I feared that I would have been the example that further emphasized why people should not come to Christ. I was ashamed of the shame I would bring to God's kingdom.

This is one reason why Christians mystify the pretense of perfection. I get it! We do not have to pretend to be perfect in order to represent a perfect God. This is false. When people see a Christian sinning, it is so alarming because that *oh so perfect* person did something they should not have done. Pretending to be perfect does not make others want to come to Christ. Instead, it pushes them away because they feel as though they are not enough to be accepted. I did not say go around telling everyone how much you sin but refuse to put on a facade to try and make people believe that you are perfect. Imperfection is what God uses. In Mark 2:17, Jesus said to them, "It is not the healthy who need a doctor, but the sick. I have not come to call the righteous, but sinners." If we were so righteous, then we would not need God.

God did not call perfect people. Being a Christian definitely does not mean that you are perfect and that you would never sin again. Instead, it means that as you journey with God and understand who He is and who He has called you to be, you sin less. Sin is not absent in the life of a true Christian, but it is lessened. When we build a relationship with God through reading, studying, and understanding his word, it changes us.

I was not only comfortable and afraid but also convinced that the people in my life were supposed to be there forever, but I was wrong. One of the biggest lies you can trick yourself into believing is that people come into your life to take up permanent residency. Too often we cling to people and things that are poisonous for us. They grew up with us, or we have known them for so long that we feel an obligation to keep them around. I experienced anxiety when God revealed it was necessary for me to get rid of some people I had connected myself to. Some of these people I had known for a while; therefore, I felt obligated to keep them around, but they were poison to my purity (whether it was mental, physical or spiritual).

When God instructed me to release my last relationship, I was both happy and scared at the same time. Happy because I needed to know this in order to move forward but scared because I had created memories that made me believe this guy would have lasted in my life. That is the danger of lack of discernment and engaging in things and people who are not sanctioned by God. I felt I could not let go because I had experienced both an emotional and spiritual connection to this person. But I prayed for direction.

We typically pray and ask God for direction when we refuse to do the last thing He told us to do. God told me to let go, but I felt the need to hold on. I was struggling and I did not understand that the very essence of my struggle was wrapped up and fabricated in the people I was connected to. I knew I needed release from these people but I constantly found excuses to hold on to them. They were poison, but the poison tasted like medicine because they suited my needs at the time. They helped me when I needed them and I could not think about what I would do or who I would call as replacements if something happened.

Many times we know that things are bad for us and still attempt to hold on regardless of how bad the infection spreads throughout our lives. There were friends and associates I needed to let go of. I knew I had to let go and to add to that, God specifically told me to rid my environment of these people but I did not listen. Until God turned up the heat and made the very presence of these people drive me crazy. The environment we sat in together was so polluted that I was suffocating. Every time I would inhale, the hairs in my nostrils would begin to burn. Being stubborn, I somehow found a way to mask the suffocation and endured the lack of oxygen. But it soon became unbearable, and I knew death was near. I cried out, "God where are you! Say something! Are you going to watch me die?"

But He gave me the answer a long time ago. The answer sat inside my obedience. My obedience to let go of the people I thought I needed but were keeping me stuck. After I accepted the obedience challenge, then and only then did God speak. Why would God give us instruction after instruction if we are reluctant to obey the first one? That is why we must be still (obedient) and listen for His voice.

Strip It Off

"Therefore, we also since we are surrounded by so great a cloud of witnesses, let us lay aside every weight, and the sin which so easily ensnares us, and let us run with endurance the race that is set before us." - Hebrews 12:1

The NLT version states it this way,

"Therefore, since we are surrounded by such a huge crowd of witnesses to the life of faith, let us strip off every weight that slows us down, especially the sin that so easily trips us up. And let us run with endurance the race God has set before us."

Hebrews clearly instructs us to strip off every weight that slows us down. Anything that causes you to sin, let it go; anything that slows down your progress, let it go. This is the perfect time to self-reflect. Evaluate your life. Ask yourself these questions: What are some things I should let go of? Who are some of the people I should sever ties with? What is in my life that is hindering me from moving forward and walking in purity? Are these songs uplifting me or do they remind me of places where I should not wish to be? These movies and shows I watch, do they push me to reflect on things contrary to edifying God? You get the idea.

Do a full analysis of every area of your life. You know what your distractions are. This can be very uncomfortable because these are things and people that you have possibly grown to love and enjoy. But the harsh reality is that if it is not serving you any purpose, you need to serve it notice. An eviction notice. There is no deliverance in comfort. Obedience is often uncomfortable. Disobedience bounds us to our place of comfort. Sever those relationships. Cut the ties and do not allow it to hold you back. Let those connections die before they call death upon you.

This reminds me of the story of Lot and his wife. God granted Lot and his wife with the opportunity to be rescued from the city of Sodom and Gomorrah. After they left the city, God gave them specific instructions:

"Flee for your lives! Don't look back, and don't stop anywhere in the plain! Flee to the mountains or you will be swept away!" (Genesis 19:17). After that, they safely settled into a small town, but Lot's wife did not follow the instructions God gave them. She looked back and became a pillar of salt. Sometimes this is us.

We receive direct instructions from God telling us what not to do and what to let go of but even in the process of being obedient, we allow disobedience to slip in. God rescued Lot's wife from such an evil city but she still could not let go. She did not strip it off; she was still tied to her past life. Tied to the comfort of what she was used to.

Holding on causes more harm than good. Much of what you might be fighting, like the depression, the addictions, the thoughts you cannot shake, directly result from the people and things you connect yourself to. Many of us are steadily fighting other people's demons. Your connection to them exposes you to their demonic influences. Don't you think you have enough of your own problems? So why would you risk your own stability just to hold on to unstable people?

Separation Anxiety

Your next level depends on what you do at this level. Our seasons last longer because we cling to what we should get rid of. When someone's time has expired in your life, your best bet is to just let it go. Their time was expired long before they entered your life because they were not supposed to be a part of your space to begin with. But thankfully we serve a God who turns everything around for our good.

The presence of these weights in your life might be the reason why you fail to access the next level of your life. What if your only lesson in this season is to dissolve that relationship? Or to call it quits with that friend with benefits? Or that best friend relationship you have with drugs and alcohol? What about pornography? Whatever it may be, that could be the one thing that is stopping your season from changing.

Stop selling yourself cheap. Some people are just not deserving of your time. They do not deserve to occupy space in your life. If you have a standard, withhold that standard because the minute you lower your standards, you lessen your value. Sometimes when we are at our lowest, we allow anything and anyone to entertain us for temporary satisfaction. They quench the thirst of our void. Esau did this. He allowed one vulnerable thirsty moment to cause him to give up his entire birthright.

Esau traded his birthright to Jacob for some stew because he was so eager to temporarily satisfy his hunger. Are you selling yourself cheap because you are hungry or thirsty? It is okay to be hungry but ensure that your hunger is being satisfied spiritually. Ensure that your decisions push you closer to God and not further away. Blessed are those who hunger and thirst for righteousness, for they will be filled (Matthew 5:6).

Would you rather gain all the pleasures of this world and lose your one soul? Luke 9:25 states, "What good is it for someone to gain the whole world, and yet lose or forfeit their very self?" It profits you none. Do not be like Esau who sought temporary fulfillment but instead let your desires rise to a place where you are fulfilled by purposeful living.

Mission Impossible

Sometimes the process of reaching spiritual purity might take longer than expected. Some of you might think, "After all of that processing, you mean to tell me that I'm still not where I need to be?" Life has a way of making you feel as if you will never progress or you will never be enough and pushes you to play the comparison game with those who seemingly have it all together. If you were to take a microscopic look at the lives of some of these people, the dangers of envy and comparison might just become your platform. Water your own grass, invest in yourself, adhere to your journey, accept your own process, and develop in your pain.

We would often hear people say that this a microwave generation. We expect everything to happen overnight; we want that Cinderella story where we click our heels together and our desires somehow magically appear before us without any effort or work. This mindset will keep you stuck forever. Anything that results in growth requires a journey of unfavorable pain.

I have experienced unfavorable pain on many occasions. I kept asking, "God, why do you keep going silent when I need you most?" Then it hit me. God is not the problem, you are! What? Yes, you are the main ingredient to your own problem. Your environment is too noisy, your heart is drifting away by each intentional wasted moment, and your spirit becomes overpowered by your flesh when you neglect to water your spirit.

We crowd our lives with toxic relationships, busyness, social outings, social media, gossip and the works. Because these things are overpowering the gentle voice of God and prompting from the Holy Spirit, our answers get lost in the noise of our lives. As we continue to miss the answers we need, our struggles are being magnified because it seems as if they will never go away. We then get upset with God because we feel like He does not care to help us. We talked about the times when God is silent but what about when He is speaking but you cannot hear Him because you turn down the volume of His voice while turning up the volume of your struggles.

In this moment, evaluate your actions, habits and practices. Are they a catalyst to your purpose or destination? Your life should be destiny and purpose focused. If your daily actions are not catapulting you toward your destiny, then make some adjustments. We look at the success of others and envy where they are at but most times we not only do not understand but also are not willing to go through their process. Everyone has a process, a journey to go through. Embrace yours and determine in your heart that you will do whatever it takes to successfully progress through your journey and obtain the rewards God has waiting for you.

Do not just focus on the rewards of your progress but instead focus on the impact you will make from being obedient to your process. Commit to the process. This means you will be determined to remain mobile. You must commit to mobility even when it feels like it is taking everything in you to do so. There is freedom in mobility. There is assurance in mobility; stagnation leads to destruction. Use the weapons that will help you fight and remain mobile so that you will always move forward.

War Weapons

Always remember that the weapons of our warfare are not carnal. We are humans but we do not wage war as humans do. We use God's mighty weapons not worldly weapons as 2 Corinthians 10:3-4 states: "For though we live in the world, we do not wage war as the world does. The weapons we fight with are not the weapons of the world. On the contrary, they have divine power to demolish strongholds."

Do not depend upon your own strength and abilities to win battles you cannot understand. God has equipped us with all the tools we need to win any battle we will ever face. But what are you using to fight your battles? The weapons granted to you by God or the world's encouragement to fight by your own strength. God has given us direct access to spiritual weapons.

Prayer, fasting, praise, worship and the whole armor of God. Your war weapons are weapons that are used to give you spiritual access. They help you fight wars unseen and always guarantee victory.

Prayer

I had an issue with prayer. I felt like my prayers were not being answered and it made no sense. But how did I pray? I prayed complaints. I complained in my communication with God. I prayed about all that went wrong rather than praying with strategy and openness to allow God to respond. I already knew my prayer would not be answered, so it only made sense to complain about my mountains. I prayed with unbelief in my heart. I prayed from a place of thinking that God already had counted me out; therefore, I had it set in my mind that my prayers would never reach His ears. Even if they reached Him, I thought I had sinned too much for Him to honor anything I requested, even deliverance. This was an erroneous and unfruitful way of thinking. Why pray if you do not expect God to hear or answer your prayers? Mark 11:24-25 (NIV) gives us instructions for our heart's posture when we pray: "Therefore I tell you, whatever you ask for in prayer, believe that you have received it, and it will be yours. And when you stand praying, if you hold anything against anyone, forgive them, so that your Father in heaven may forgive you your sins." There you have it. Forgive, Believe, Pray.

What you pray also makes a difference. Pray specific and strategic prayers. "Thank you God for waking me up this morning, starting me on my way clothing me in my right mind . . . amen" is not the type of prayer that will help you tear down strongholds and overcome temptations. It is a prayer of gratitude toward God and nothing is wrong with it. But if you are searching for deliverance and help to triumph over struggles, you need an approach just for that. Effective prayer. Pray asking God to give you the strength to overcome temptations. More than anything, find the scriptures that speak to what you are dealing with and pray those scriptures. The word has power; the word has your answers. Pray using the solution not the problem.

Fasting

This was always uncomfortable for me, as it probably is for many, and in the moments when I needed it most, it did not seem to work. But why? I fasted because I was told to. I did not do it because I needed to and this is the main reason it failed. I did not properly exercise it. Here comes that word again: strategy. I went into a time of fasting hoping for God to tell me in His deep voice how I would overcome my then soul tie. I wanted answers with no seeking, no effort, and no true sacrifice.

Fasting puts your flesh under subjection to the needs of your spirit. Fasting is a way of overpowering your fleshly desires to satisfy your spiritual needs and seek the answers that are the catalyst for your breakthrough. Naturally you realize that you have been struggling for too long and you have tried but you continuously failed because you do not have the answers. Fasting helps you set aside your wants (food, enjoyment, etc.) to have your needs supplied.

Desperation pushed me to fast and seek God in a deeper way for my deliverance. I was tired and exhausted from fighting to overcome my struggles of impurities and constantly losing the battle. I always ended up back to square one. I needed real answers. The question is, however, are you desperate enough to see deliverance and change?

Praise and Worship

It is very difficult to sing praises and send up worship when life does not seem favorable to you but this is when it is necessary–when you do not feel like it. Pushing past your reality to honor God is a sacrifice. Making this a habit will be very beneficial to you. It will fuel you even in your difficult seasons.

They are weapons. When the enemy thought he took you out, but sees you lifting hands in worship, he does not know what to do. It confuses him and his plans. 2 Chronicles 20:22 reads, "At the very moment they began to sing and give praise, the LORD caused the armies of Ammon, Moab, and Mount Seir to start fighting among themselves."

> "True worship is a valuing or a treasuring of God above all things" (Desiring God)[3]

Worship is a posture of the heart. It engages your heart to connect with God in exaltation of His holy name and being. When you can push aside your shortcomings, disappointments, trails and struggles and express to God His worth, sovereignty and power, you are truly worshipping. It should be unconditional. It is a weapon that helps us tap into the true essence of who God is through acknowledging that He is bigger than what our current realities might be.

---

[3] Source: https://www.desiringgod.org/interviews/what-is-worship

The Armor of God

You cannot go into war unprepared, yet expecting that you will win. You need your full armor.

"Stand therefore, having girded your waist with truth, having put on the breastplate of righteousness, and having shod your feet with the preparation of the gospel of peace; above all, taking the shield of faith with which you will be able to quench all the fiery darts of the wicked one. And take the helmet of salvation, and the sword of the Spirit, which is the word of God."
- Ephesians 6:14-17

The word has all the answers you need. I realized this after moving from just reading the word to studying it and applying it to my life. Once you begin to practice and implement these war weapons, you will be on the right track. You are now in progress to changing and developing your heart. In doing so, your posture changes. You become postured for victory.

Postured for Victory

Past failures and future predictions cause us to lose focus. But you have war weapons that reposition and posture you. If you accept defeat, then defeat will be your portion but if you cling onto God, His promises will be your lifestyle. You can access His promises by using your war weapons; the word is your guide. Do not allow your past to dictate your posture.

Stop allowing the negativity of your past to distract and hinder you from God's reality. Stop disqualifying yourself when God has qualified you long before your mistakes while still knowing you would make them.

Remember the following verses:

"No, dear brothers and sisters, I have not achieved it, but I focus on this one thing: Forgetting the past and looking forward to what lies ahead." - Philippians 3:13-14

"Let your eyes look directly ahead and let your gaze be fixed straight in front of you. Watch the path of your feet and all your ways will be established."

- Proverbs 4:25-27

Like God did with King Solomon, He will do with us: "Solomon asked for wisdom and God granted him his request and he also said that he will give him the things that he didn't ask for wealth honor and long life if he's obedient" (1 Kings 3). God saw the sincerity of Solomon's heart. He was not interested in personal gain but in his calling. He wanted to function effectively in the place where God had called him–to the throne as king. He was a great leader to God's people because he knew it was not about him but about his purpose.

See yourself in the way God sees you. He desires for us to see that our purpose is for the honor and glory of His kingdom. If we function in that mindset, then He will not withhold anything from us because like with Solomon, He will see the sincerity of our heart to want to function effectively in our purposes. God wants us to proficiently carry out His works. Seek first the kingdom of God and His righteousness and all other things will be added. Seeking the kingdom gives you understanding. We want what He adds but often refuse to seek Him first.

Prayer

Father give me continued hope in your ability and desire to renew my character. Help me understand that even though the enemy is continuously after my life, you are ever present, even in the moments when I fall. Assure me that your mission is always possible. You will fulfill your purpose for my life. My mistakes, God, use them as propellers that push me closer toward my destiny. Teach me to war, as I now understand that much of what I deal with requires spiritual strategies to overcome. I trust you to fight every battle with me because with you I know that I can win and will never lose.

Genetically Modified

There are many battles that are never revealed to the natural eye. We often go through storms in life and many times we cannot make the connection that would help us understand why we are going through these storms. Some battles are natural–those that we can make practical connections to–other battles are spiritual.

There is the natural realm and the spirit realm. The natural realm operates by the five senses but only God can give insight into the spirit realm. Sometimes it is difficult to understand this spirit realm we speak of, but this is where the importance of being in tune with God comes in. As we draw closer to God, He reveals to us that which we cannot know or even begin to comprehend. God uses His Holy Spirit to give us wisdom and insight. Insight into what is taking place in the spiritual realm while giving us the strategies we need to equip ourselves for spiritual battles. He helps us make spiritual connections to the trials we are experiencing naturally. Sometimes the mental trauma, the unexplained emotional discourse, the unexplained depression, are only the manifestation of the war that is going on in the spirit realm concerning your life.

The following scriptures explain the spirit realm better than I ever could:

"The Spirit searches all things, even the deep things of God. For who knows a person's thoughts except their own spirit within them? In the same way no one knows the thoughts of God except the Spirit of God. What we have received is not the spirit of the world, but the Spirit who is from God, so that we may understand what God has freely given us. This is what we speak, not in words taught to us by human wisdom but in words taught by the Spirit, explaining spiritual realities with Spirit-taught words. The person without the Spirit does not accept the things that come from the Spirit of God but considers them foolishness, and cannot understand them because they are discerned only through the Spirit. The person with the Spirit makes judgments about all things, but such a person is not subject to merely human judgments." - 1 Corinthians 2:10-15

"For our struggle is not against flesh and blood, but against the rulers, against the authorities, against the powers of this dark world and against the spiritual forces of evil in the heavenly realms." - Ephesians 6:12

"This is what we speak, not in words taught us by human wisdom but in words taught by the Spirit, explaining spiritual realities with Spirit-taught words. The person without the Spirit does not accept the things that come from the Spirit of God but considers them foolishness, and cannot understand them because they are discerned only through the Spirit."
- 1 Corinthians 2:13-14

Your genes carry information that passed on to you from your parents, grandparents, great grandparents, great great grandparents, great great

great grandparents, you get the point. Some of your habits, behaviors and struggles result from the decisions that these family members have made and the sins they have committed. Sometimes you wonder why you have strange desires and habits that you cannot seem to shake. It might just be something that has been linked to your family for generations.

Sometimes we struggle with things we could never determine the origin of. There may have been pitfalls you dealt with because of the generational curses that have traveled through your bloodline. The addictions you have encountered are not by happenstance. Maybe it is the same thing that your great grandmother dealt with that trickled straight down to you. Just because it traveled through past generations does not mean you have to carry it.

I can point out a few generational curses in my family. One of them is a lack of display of love. Love and affection was not shown, neither was it verbalized. A display of love and affection was not something I was used to seeing both in my immediate and extended family. It seemed as if they thought their presence was enough, or the fact that they provided monetarily and materialistically. This distorted my view of love, affection and communication. I assumed that people knew you loved them by your presence and the things you gave them. This affected how I handled my relationships.

Verbalizing my affection was null and void; that was the hardest and strangest thing for me. Saying "I love you" was uncomfortable for me. It was straining to say the least. Like really, how do I say those words? How do I tell my mother I love her? My father? My siblings? It just felt so strange. I wondered how they would respond. Would they look at me as being overly emotional? What if they did not say it back?

I withheld affection because that was the norm that was quietly preached in our family. I remember randomly trying to tell my parents that I loved them at the end of our phone conversations (I lived away from them so this was our way of communicating) and it felt abnormal. But God helped me overcome the old and ill feelings while He established new norms.

God has modified my genes. I am still a part of my family but He has created new habits that will travel through generations after me. He modified through restoration so that I would not be a carrier of any more curses. It is still a journey to walk into the newness of God but I can assure you that it is already done. My genes have already been modified for my children to carry and my children's children and their children forever. The same is possible for you. You can be the agent that activates change for your bloodline.

Spiritual battles are real and if you are keen in developing an effective action plan, then change is the thing for you. We can conquer if we know who we are and act upon it. There is a practical action plan that I used to counteract the transference of a generational curse away from me and my future children. I chose not only to show but also to verbalize love.

A practical action plan is necessary to help combat generational curses along with the war weapons previously mentioned. At the end of this chapter, there is a space where you can write out steps toward your action plan.

GENETICALLY MODIFIED

The practical steps I took were to:

Know Your Identify

Knowing who you are and what you came from. Identify the curse. Sometimes generational curses go unnoticed because they seem like the norm. Look at the trends in your family that are sins: alcoholism, drug abuse, poverty, lack of educational advancement, complacency, pregnancy outside of marriage, unfaithfulness, lack of self-control, divorce, greed, hereditary sickness (cancer, diabetes, etc.), barrenness, etc. All of these can be examples of generational curses and are very prevalent in our world today. There are so many.

Discover what curses have lodged in your family line. Write them down. This is the first step. People often talk about breaking generational curses and walking in freedom and healing. You cannot be free from something that you do not know you are bound to. In the same way, you cannot break or overcome something you do not know exists.

Repent and Forgive

Repent of the curse. You might say, "Oh, it's not my fault. Why must I repent for something I am not the cause of?" While you are not the initiator of the curse, your acceptance to it caused you to be a carrier. This means that even though it may be a struggle for your family, you did not have to carry on the trend. It was not forced on you. You subconsciously, willingly, engaged. This is why you must repent. Repentance is the gateway to freedom. Repentance is for you. Our goal is to walk in freedom and create healthy norms for the generations that will follow us.

Forgiveness is not for the other person but for you instead. It is so that you can be free. Forgive your family for passing the curse on to you. For years I had blamed my dad for being an emotionally dead person. I needed him to get it together so that I, too, could get it together. He was the reason I sought love from so many places and from so many people anyway, right? Therefore, I needed him to fix it! But no! How could I blame him for something he thought was a norm?

That's all he knew, so he displayed his love to my siblings and I in the best way he knew how. Whether that was good enough for me did not matter. I needed to realize that he did his best. He may not have broken the curse, but he tried his best to be effective. I had to realize that maybe he did not even think of it as being a curse because it is such a family norm. I had to get over myself. I had to decide that I would forgive so that I could move forward and create the change that my family needs. I initiated the spark of change.

Substitute

Substitute bad for good. Find scriptures that counteract the bad. Find phrases or words you can repeat daily to retrain your mind. What are some new habits that you can practice? The goal is to find a good solution for whatever bad that is present. Create new godly norms. Surround yourself with people who can help you.

God strategically placed my accountability sisters in my life. They have helped me in more ways than I can express. They would often express their appreciation and love for me. They made this a norm and that drew me to want to be more emotionally expressive. I learned that expressing yourself does not have to be a strain nor is it taboo. People love to know how you feel. My sisters set the foundation of emotional safety for me. Not only are they open to expressing love, but also they have taught me how to share my opinion without the fear of being ridiculed or outcast.

Take Action

You can implement your own action plan. Be sure to make your plan a daily practice. Be intentional about successfully living out the plan that you implement. My sisters are intentional about ensuring that we are each other's safety net. We have made it a habit to check in with one another, uplift, pray, fast and develop together. No one gets left behind. Maybe a community is what you need. Accountability is important.

GENETICALLY MODIFIED

You have the power to initiate and establish change. You can alter the trajectory of your generation by breaking the generational curses that have attached themselves to your family name. The Bible states in Genesis 20:5-6, ". . . I, the LORD your God, am a jealous God, punishing the children for the sin of the parents to the third and fourth generation of those who hate me, but showing love to a thousand generations of those who love me and keep my commandments."

When you repent of your own sin, and ask God for mercy on behalf of the sins of your ancestors, God is faithful to break the generational curse. But YOU have to make the decision to turn your life around and separate yourself from the past identity of sin. Your decision to change your life and live a life of complete obedience and surrender will bless thousands of generations after you, as according to the quoted scripture.

That is the grace and favor that is available to us. It could affect thousands of generations after you. God will grant you the grace and strength that you need to break generational curses and create new godly habits.

Godly habits that you will be able to pass down to your children and they to their children. The goal is to transfer generational blessings rather than generational curses. It is possible! Grace is available to us.

God's grace is greater than any punishment we will ever face. The grace for generations to come is greater than the battle you are facing today. There is no sin that God cannot forgive. There is nothing you or your family can do to count you out of the purpose that God has for you once you submit to Him.

not miss the chance to be the initiator of generational transformation. You can stop generational curses by being the first catalyst of change in your bloodline. Change is not inevitable; it must be intentional. Are you willing to be intentional about your change? Call it a necessary purity transformation. This change begins on the inside; it is a transformation of the heart, the formation into the beautiful pearl that God has intended you to have. This should be our heart's cry as according to Psalm 51:10, "Create in me a clean heart, O God; and renew a right spirit within me."

GENETICALLY MODIFIED

I desired for God to cleanse me of my filth and make my life anew and I achieved just that and more.

Breaking the Curse

Identify the curse

_____

_____

_____

_____

_____

Repent and Forgive

What do you have to repent of? Who must you forgive? Who did you blame for your struggles?

_____

_____

_____

_____

_____

_____

Genetically Modified

Substitute

Bad (Generational curse)	Good (Scripture, new habits, affirming words, etc.)

Take Action

How are you going to implement the good that you wrote down? How will you create new habits?

_____

_____

_____

_____

_____

_____

Remembering Grace

Grace is a word that people carelessly use every day. I say "carelessly" because we assume people know what it means when many times we ourselves don't. There is much more to grace than the surface context we use it in. This entire chapter is about remembering this thing called grace you have divine access to. But it is difficult to remember grace when we do not even understand what it is. To remember grace, we must understand grace. We have access to grace through the work of the crucifixion and the resurrection. God made the biggest sacrifice for us by sending Jesus to be crucified. He carried the weight of sin for all of us. Jesus was all God had and He freely gave Him to us.

    I did not understand what this thing called grace was or how it could help me. I did not understand grace during my journey and truthfully, I am still trying to grasp the concept behind grace. Sometimes it is difficult to understand that God's love is unconditional.

I know my downfalls, my shortcomings, and the sins I have committed. God knows even more about me than I know about myself, yet He remains the same. He does not turn His back on us nor forsake us, even when we intentionally sin against Him. Even when we argue and fuss with Him because things do not go our way, He does not change His ways toward us. He knows how unsteady we are. His desires and plans for our lives exist beyond our insufficiencies. When we leave Him, He is willing to leave the ninety-nine to run after us. He is a good, good father. Words cannot describe Him. His ways are perfect and He never fails us. Remember: "God showed his great love for us by sending Christ to die for us while we were still sinners." (Romans 5:8)

God has unrestrictedly given us grace to be used in so many instances, for many reasons. Grace is favor granted to the undeserved despite our sinful nature. God knew we would be born into sin, yet His ways toward us does not change. He knew you would need Him to grant you favor in and out of every season. That is the power behind grace. It grants you what you need even when you do not deserve it. There is nothing you or I could ever do to earn this because we do not deserve it (Isaiah 64:7). God's love is a free gift (Romans 3:24). You cannot pay for it.

What an amazing God we serve, right? He looks after the needs of His people regardless of what their positions might be. Unqualified, rich, poor, educated, uneducated, drug addict, sex addict, perverted mind, thief or whatever it might be, it does not disqualify you from accessing the grace of God. God can use you in whatever state you are in. The word states, "those who are well have no need of a physician, but those who are sick" (Matthew 9:12).

Therefore, if you fall into one of the descriptions previously mentioned, that qualifies you for access to the greatest physician because you are sick with sin. Grace gives you that unmerited access. God Himself is grace. Without Him we can do nothing but with Him we can do anything; we can do all things through him who gives us strength (Philippians 4:13).

Infused throughout the Bible are the different effects of grace. These examples can help us understand what the immeasurable grace of God looks like.

I will share some below:

"For it is by grace you have been saved, through faith— and this is not from yourselves, it is the gift of God."
- Ephesians 2:8-9

"By grace through faith God saves us. We don't deserve to be saved but by God's grace salvation is freely available to us. God in his grace freely makes us right in his sight." - Romans 3:24

"He saved us and called us to live a holy life. He did this not because of our own qualities, but because that was his plan from the beginning of time-to show us his grace through Jesus Christ." - 2 Timothy 1:9

God sacrificed His only son, Jesus Christ, as a means of a gateway for sinners to access heaven. That is an act of extreme grace. Before that we were in bondage to sin. Salvation grants us freedom. Salvation is not possible any other way than through Jesus. We can read Jesus' words from the Bible in John 14:6 which reads, "I am the way and the truth and the life. No one comes to the Father except through me." Jesus stood in the gap for us. He is the bridge between God and man. It is because of Him that God has grace on us.

Grace overpowers sin. Sin puts us in unprofitable conditions. Many times we feel so dirty and filthy because of the sin we have committed. We feel as if we are so far away from God, because of our sin, that we cannot ever access Him again. This feeling of not being worthy of going back to God takes over. That is the effect of sin. But thankfully grace grants the ability to triumph over sin and death through Jesus Christ (Romans 5:17).

Think about the significance of the following scriptures:

"Just as sin ruled over all people and brought them to death, now God's wonderful grace rules instead, giving us right standing with God resulting in eternal life through Jesus Christ our Lord." - Romans 5:20

"This journey is so amazing. We see Jesus who was made a little lower than angels, for the suffering of death crowned with glory and honor, that he, by the grace of God might taste death for everyone."
- Hebrews 2:9

    God was so concerned about us being able to overcome sin through Him that His very own son was demoted (a little lower than angels) so that He could suffer and taste death just for you. The pressures of sin rested upon Him. All that we did and will ever sinfully do rested on Jesus while He hung on that cross. Through the taste of death and resurrection power, sin lost its grip on you. Sin used to hold you hostage but through the resurrection all chains were broken, and grace was all the more activated for us. The sting of death is sin (1 Corinthians 15:56). So, Jesus had to overcome death in order for us to have victory. All of this speaks of God's undeserved grace that He extends toward us daily. Now think about it, what have you done to qualify you for that kind of love?

Grace grants freedom and restores. Through salvation and overpowering sin, we see how we are granted freedom through grace. As Romans 6:14 states, "For sin shall not have dominion over you, for you are not under the law but under grace." The work of the cross made you free. We often feel stuck and immovable because we do not understand what we have access to neither do we understand the magnitude of the sacrifice that God made for us.

Sin put us in a place where we feel like there is no way out. A feeling of being caged in and surrounded by darkness. All it takes is light to make darkness nonexistent. There is no limit to what you can accomplish in Jesus. That is why the scriptures state in Philippians 4:13, "I can do all things through Christ who strengthens me." The lies that develop as a residue of sin attempt to dictate otherwise to you. Believe truth only.

Grace strengthens. As Hebrews 13:9 states, "Do not be carried away by all kinds of strange teachings. It is good for our hearts to be strengthened by grace, not by eating ceremonial foods, which is of no benefit to those who do so."

After sinning repeatedly, I did not think I would make it out of the state I was in. I walked around slumped because of the severe amount of weakness I felt. I felt severely drained, with no energy or hope for restoration. But thank God for grace that strengthens. After willingly being immersed in impurity grace not only saved me but also gave me the strength to overcome myself and walk away from what tried to kill me. I was my greatest enemy as I fought against my flesh. Grace brought me boxing gloves, the daily dose of protein and carbohydrates, and the extra muscle mass I needed to win my fight.

Grace is sufficient. Even when it seems as if the things before me are not enough, I often remind myself,

"My grace is sufficient for thee: for my strength is made perfect in weakness. Most gladly therefore will I rather glory in my infirmities, that the power of Christ may rest upon me" (2 Corinthians 12:9).

Grace saved me. While I was down-and-out, grace kept me when I did not want to be kept. Grace reached down in the pits of darkness for me and illuminated a new light in me. Grace kept me alive when the enemy thought he could have celebrated my death. Grace.

Our state does not determine His grace. His grace remains consistent regardless of what position we are in. His grace was present in the midst of all your actions you deemed made you impure. Grace…grace…grace.

The Crowning

Crowns are precious commodities. A queen does not have to wear her crown at all times, yet she is and will always be recognized. Her life exudes her position of authority by her actions and the purpose she carries. She knows what she represents and displays it with or without the appearance of a physical crown. Think of your crown as your life. There are two options: either you choose to continuously live in a place of emptiness because of the things that have happened in your life or you decide that you will change your heart's posture.

In choosing to change your heart, you will be postured with an unwavering commitment to stick through all seasons. Not only sticking through seasons but learning and growing through your pain. As your heart is tested and refined as gold, you will have a heart that matches your crown as a precious daughter of the King. This is where my inspiration for the book cover came from. The gold represents the quality of our heart when we begin to apply strategies of purity to our lives. God begins to do a work inside of us, creating in us a clean heart and renewing a right spirit within us. (Psalm 51:10)

God creates masterpieces from what you or others might think is only dirt and pain. God is earnestly waiting to give you a renewed and restored heart so that you can experience the most beautiful crown (life). A satisfying, abundant life. God delights in the welfare of his servants (Psalm 35:27). It pleases Him when we prosper; He is concerned about His people.

Your heart is the pearl of your life. To live a crowned life, you must accept that the process your pearl (heart) goes through is a symbol of memories, purpose, and success.

When God gave me the title for this book, I did not realize how much revelation I would receive from it. In studying, I have discovered a very interesting fact about pearls. Pearls form when a particle becomes trapped in an oyster. The pearls are made as a form of relief from pain. This is exactly how God wants us to view our difficulties—with the confidence that something beautiful will be the result. I hated my difficult seasons. I could not see the light of day in those dark seasons but I now understand why they were necessary.

We must understand and know that God causes everything to work together for our good because we love Him and are called according to His purpose (Romans 8:28). We all have a call on our lives but the devil tries to distract us with the negativity and downfalls in our lives when in reality God's intent is to use our shortcomings for His glory. Life would be much more satisfying if we began to view our pains as pearls. If an oyster can mask its pain by creating something beautiful, then why is it that we refuse daily to trust and believe that God is creating valuable pearls for us?

Memories

The painful process that your heart had to go through is now a memory. The memories of the heartache you endured remains. We tend to focus on things that are not going right and complain; but we forget that even though we are not where we desire to be, we are far better than we used to be. Remember when you almost committed suicide? God rescued you. You were supposed to, like me, be dead now but you were given another chance at fulfilling your purpose in life. Remember when you almost lost your mind? Remember when you were battered and wounded by the people you loved most? You overcame! If you have not yet overcome in these areas or in any other difficult area in your life, know that the pearls are waiting for you to claim them. You can overcome! One day it will all be a memory that you will use as a testimony not only for yourself but also for others.

We do not give ourselves enough credit for our progress. We too often look at other people's lives and use that as a measuring stick for our own lives. Your journey is different. Your process is different. Your memories serve a different purpose. Give yourself the credit you deserve for the hard work and heart work you went through to successfully get to where you are. Allow your memories, whether good or bad, to propel you.

They keep you assured that God is with you. In seasons to come, or even in your present state, if you are feeling like God has left and does not care about you, remember that He has brought you out before. He will definitely do it again. You have the pearls, the new heart posture, to prove it. The situation might change and the intensity of your fight might be greater but one thing you can be sure of is that God is consistent. He always remains the same.

Memories should give you more strength. Remember the last thing you went through that you thought you wouldn't make it out of. Maybe it was a divorce, a toxic relationship, an addiction, a season of financial lack, or the pressures of not thinking you would make it out of school successfully, or whatever it might have been. Remember that season? Right! God brought you out; you did not die there. I never thought I would finish university, but I completed it successfully. Surprisingly enough, I am ready to go back once again. Isn't that uplifting? I am ready to conquer the same thing I was afraid I would never make it through and at an even higher level that requires more work. I am confident I will be successful once again when I return.

God gave you overcoming power. The way you overcame might not look favorable in your eyes, but He still gave you the strength and power to overcome. Use that strength from the memory of the last thing you overcame to give you the fuel to move forward. Life is full of obstacles but they are only there to make you stronger.

Purpose

Your pearl (heart) symbolizes your life's purpose. God allows us to experience situations to help expose matters of the heart. As these matters are exposed, He places us in environments that deal with our hearts, aid in growth, and propel us toward purpose. He gives us the power to overcome. God established your purpose long ago. You must decide to fulfill it by the choices you make in your life. You choose to or not to remain the clay in the hand of the ready potter (God).

Allow Him to mold your heart into what He intended so that your crown (life) will be perfected. Allow Him to add the heat necessary to shape the frame of your crown. Allow Him to add the jewels, the pearls that will add to the value of your crown. Your purpose depends on it.

Vow

Sometimes the biggest hindrance in your life is you. We talk ourselves out of victories because life becomes too hard or because we have failed so many times. I talked myself out living a life of purity. Yes! Because it took too much effort and energy. I also thought I was incapable of successfully living a life of purity because I fell so many times; I got it wrong so many times it seemed impossible.

I talked myself into failure because I did not think I could be successful in this area of my life. That was exactly where the enemy wanted me, in a space where I discouraged myself. Make the vow today that even in your pain, you will remain in God's hand. Vow to accept your process in order to progress. That you will remember the end goal will be a crown (life) that pleases God. Let that vow become engraved in your heart

Vow never to turn back or go back to a place of being stuck because you have moved away from God. Keep moving. You do this by staying at the feet of Jesus. Living a life of total surrender and submission to whatever God's will for your life may be. Never mind your mistakes and imperfections; He uses those to help shape you into your purpose. Vow not to give into the tactics nor entertain the distractions of Satan. Commit to the process of purpose and purity.

Success

Your pearl (heart) is a memoir of your success. You have successfully broke the cycles that had you bound. If this has not happened for you yet, do not be discouraged; your memoir is still being written. You are building your portfolio. God is in the business of doing strategic heart work. Growth and development are important parts of that portfolio. Like the pearl, we grow through pain. It is almost never pleasing until you experience the results. Do not focus on the pain but remember to learn in the furnace. While you are going through, grow through. If you cling to your journey, then success will be inevitable.

Do not get to a place of complacency because you have experienced success. Take care of your pearls. Put your lesson to use. Success is just an indicator of your progress, not *the* progress.

Genesis

Genesis means origin.

It does not end here. In fact, it is just the beginning, the genesis to your future successes. Never go back to your genesis, to your beginning, but always remember it. In the actual book of Genesis is the premise of the earth, of existence. The earth does not go back and repeat its inception phase. Your genesis should be referenced not repeated. We refer to the stories in the book of Genesis that took place and we use them for understanding and guidance. Treat your life the same way.

In dealing with any issue and problem, always refer to the origin of which that thing emerged. Every issue has an origin. It would be wise to address the issue from where it has been established rather than grabbing it at the end and attempting to work your way backwards. Forward momentum is what you need for success. Continuous progression, growth and self-development should be your priority.

My heart's desire is that we all win. Win the fight of the constant battle between impurity and purity, which is ultimately the fight between flesh and spirit. The battleground is the heart. It is possible but always remember it is a daily fight. Every day you are in a battle; always remain conscious of this. We lose because we are not only unaware but also ill prepared. Awareness brings preparation. No one willingly goes into a battle unprepared.

If you have had an experience similar to mine or one you think is worse, I pray that this book has encouraged you to move beyond a place of feeling that there is no turnaround to a place of complete restoration where you, too, can celebrate your purity success. It is definitely not a destination but a lifelong journey that requires great intentionality and consistency. Purity is heart work. Allow God to work on your heart so that He can open your mind, body and soul to a life that is pure and free.

www.ingramcontent.com/pod-product-compliance
Lightning Source LLC
Chambersburg PA
CBHW070559010526
44118CB00012B/1376